CREATING A HOME

CURTAINS & SOFT FURNISHINGS

WARD LOCK

CONTENTS

© Ward Lock Limited, 1988

Villiers House, 41-47 Strand, London, WC2N 5JE, a Cassell Company

Reprinted 1989, 1990

Based on *Creating A Home,*

First Edition © Eaglemoss Publications Limited, 1986.

ISBN 0 7063 6728 6

Printed in Great Britain by Cooper Clegg Limited

INTRODUCTION

This book is a must for every home-maker who isn't satisfied with the mass-produced uniformity of ready-made curtains and shop-bought soft furnishings. Even if you have never made the simplest of curtains or a plain cushion cover before, it will soon give you the confidence to try your hand at elaborate styles. Full-colour photographs illustrate the effects you can achieve, and step-by-step captioned drawings show exactly how to create them for yourself.

Curtains and Soft Furnishings starts with a section on window treatments, with instructions for making basic curtains, unlined and lined, also lace and sheer curtains, and economical café curtains. Then come different ways of dressing up any curtain style, with pelmets, valances, tiebacks, swags and tails, all with detailed step-by-step instructions. In addition, there are illustrated guides to choosing the right type of curtains for particular windows, choosing curtain fabrics, tracks and poles, and dealing with problem windows.

Some windows look better with blinds, and step-by-step instructions are given for making three different kinds: plain roller blinds, and the pleated and softly gathered ones known as Roman and Austrian blinds. Also included is an illustrated guide to buying blinds and shutters of all types.

The soft furnishings section begins with step-by-step instructions for making cushions and cushion trims, continues with simple lampshades and finishes with how to make loose covers for anything from a dining chair to a three-piece suite.

Curtains and Soft Furnishings will help you create elegant tailor-made curtains and soft furnishings which look as if they were commissioned from an interior decorator.

SIMPLE UNLINED CURTAINS

Unlined curtains involve a minimum of sewing and are simple to make up. Detachable linings are easily added to unlined curtains.

Unlined curtains are ideal for use in kitchens, bathrooms and playrooms, or on any window where insulation and light exclusion are less important than easy laundering and versatility. Use sheer fabrics to filter harsh sunlight, or try decorative lace over a simple practical blind that can be pulled down for warmth and privacy.

Detachable linings added to cotton curtains will shut out more light and provide better insulation. They can also be washed separately from the main curtain.

The technique for making unlined curtains is basic to making any curtain. Curtain tape attached to the top has slits for the hooks from which the curtain hangs on a track or pole.

Measuring up Before measuring for curtains, it is essential to fix the track or pole in place so that the exact height and width can be taken. The track or pole is fixed in the window recess or outside the recess and just above the frame. If it is outside the recess it should extend, if possible, at least 15cm/6in on each side of the frame so that the curtains can be fully drawn back from the glass for maximum daylight. The height of the pole will depend on the curtain length you choose.

What length curtains? Curtain lengths fall into three categories: sill length, just below sill length (clearing the top of a radiator, for example), and floor length. The length you choose depends on the size and shape of the window, your style of furnishings and the visual effect you want.

Choosing heading tape The type of heading tape you choose will influence the 'look' of your curtains, and determine the width of fabric needed. Standard heading tape is economical on fabric and gives a softly gathered, even fullness suitable for lightweight, unlined curtains.

Smart stripes
A simple unlined curtain with softly gathered pencil pleating is a good choice for this neat bathroom. It is quick to make and easy to wash.

Heading tapes for more tailored pencil or pinch pleats require more fabric. A special heading tape is available for detachable linings, and can be used with any decorative curtain heading.

Use synthetic fibre tape for sheer and synthetic fabrics, cotton tape for natural fabrics.

Choosing fabric Lightweight and sheer furnishing fabrics are ideal for unlined curtains. Cottons, either plain or printed offer the widest colour range. There is also a wide range of semi-transparent fabrics, usually in synthetic fibres, from fine net and voile to heavier lace designs and open weaves.

If possible buy fabric that is wide enough to make up a curtain without having to make seams. To work out how much fabric you need, see overleaf.

Pattern repeats Plain fabrics and small prints are the best choice for a beginner; avoid large patterns and horizontal stripes which need extra care in cutting and matching up. Pattern matching is covered in detail on page 13.

Sewing thread The sewing thread should match the fibre content of your fabric. Polyester thread is best for synthetics, cotton for natural fabrics.

CHECK YOUR NEEDS

Curtain fabric
- ☐ Curtain heading tape
- ☐ Curtain hooks

Lining fabric
- ☐ Lining heading tape
- ☐ Curtain hooks

Plus:
- ☐ Steel tape (to measure window)
- ☐ Calculator (optional)
- ☐ Scissors
- ☐ Tape measure
- ☐ Pins
- ☐ Needles
- ☐ Matching sewing thread
- ☐ Sewing machine
- ☐ Iron and ironing board

HOW MUCH FABRIC DO YOU NEED?

Use this method of calculating the total amount of fabric needed for all curtains, lined and unlined. A pocket calculator may be helpful.

To get the width, measure the length of the track or pole and multiply by at least 1½-2 times for standard heading tape (by up to 3 times for other heading tapes – check manufacturer's instructions).

Add 2.5cm for each side hem allowance (5cm for sheers).

Add 10-15cm to each curtain width if the curtains are to overlap on a crossover arm at the centre.

Divide the total figure by the width of your fabric to give the number of fabric widths needed. Round up to the next full width if necessary.

To get the length, measure from curtain track or pole to the desired length (sill, radiator or floor). Add 4cm for top hem (for standard heading tape) and 15cm for bottom hem. Double the hem allowances for sheer fabrics.

To get the total amount multiply this figure by the number of fabric widths. This quantity of fabric is then divided between the number of curtains required.

☐ If the fabric has a pattern repeat, add one full pattern repeat per fabric width.
☐ If washable fabric is likely to shrink, buy an extra 10cm per metre. Either wash the fabric before cutting out or make up with all the excess in the bottom hem. The curtain can then be let down after the first wash.

1 Cut out the fabric
Lay the fabric flat on a large table if you have one, or clear an area of floor space to work on.

Curtains will not hang properly unless you start with a straight cut across the width. If the fabric has a straight thread pattern across the width, pull out a thread as a guide for a straight cutting line. Otherwise cut at a right angle to the selvedges. Line up the pattern repeat, if necessary, before cutting subsequent widths.

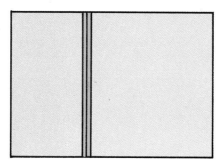 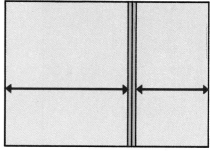

2 Join fabric widths △
If the fabric is narrower than the curtain width, make up the required width by adding a strip of fabric to the outside edge.

3 Stitch the seams ▷
Using a simple flat seam, pin the two pieces of fabric together with right sides facing and edges and pattern matching. Tack and stitch 1.5cm from edges. Remove tacking and press seam open. To prevent puckering, clip into the seam allowance (particularly if it is a selvedge) every 10cm along the edges.

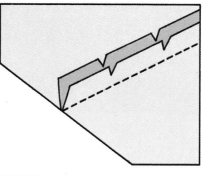

4 Stitch side hems ▷
Turn 5mm of the allowance to the wrong side and press. Fold remaining 2cm of hem allowance to the wrong side and tack. Then machine or slipstitch through all the layers.

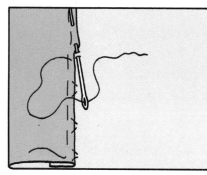

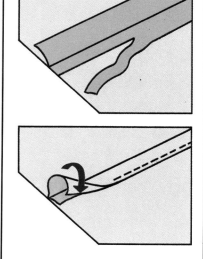

DELICATE FABRICS
If the fabric is likely to fray or you want a neater finish, turn this flat seam into a flat fell seam. Trim off half one seam allowance, then fold the other seam allowance over it to enclose the raw edges. Tack and topstitch through all the layers. This stitching line will show through on the right side of the fabric.

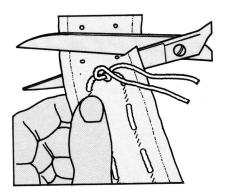

5 *Prepare the heading tape* △
Cut a length of heading tape to the finished width of the curtain plus 8cm (for neatening the ends). At the end where the curtains will meet or overlap, pull 4cm of each cord free on the wrong side of the tape and knot securely.

Trim off surplus tape 1.5cm away from the knot; press this surplus to the wrong side. At the other end of the tape, ease out 4cm of each cord on the right side. Turn surplus tape to wrong side and press.

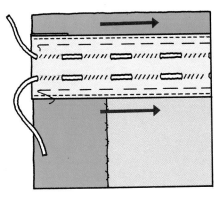

6 *Attach heading tape* △
At the top of the curtain turn 4cm to the wrong side and press. Position tape on the wrong side of the curtain to cover raw hem edge, with top edge of tape no more than 2.5cm below the top and the loose tape cords on the outer edge of the curtain. Tack the tape in place. Machine stitch both long edges of tape in the same direction to prevent puckering; stitch across the short knotted end of tape. Remove tacking.

7 *Gather curtain heading* ▷
Holding the loose cords together, gather the fabric until fully pleated, easing out evenly until the right width. Tie the cords together, and tuck out of sight; don't cut them as they are needed to release the curtain fullness for cleaning. Insert hooks at about 8cm intervals all along the tape.

TIPS FOR SEWING SHEER FABRICS
Seams, particularly in fine nets, tend to be very obvious against the light of a window so avoid making joins if possible. If one fabric width is too narrow for your window, make up separate curtains to hang side by side – or simply hang widths without sewing – allowing the fullness of the curtain to hide the overlapping edges. If you do join widths, a flat fell seam (see opposite) or french seam makes a neat finish. Very fine lacy sheers should be overlapped to match the shape of the design and seamed by hand.

Finish sheer fabrics with machined

Cool, white and light
Full-length sheer curtains with a delicate pattern are teamed with white painted shutters which are closed for privacy at night.

double hems to look neat and prevent raw edges from showing through – use a special translucent synthetic fibre tape made specifically for sheers and nets. A double hem at the top will mask the outline of heading tape. Take care when turning hems on open weave fabrics to match up the weave and ensure a maximum of solid pattern area to sew through.

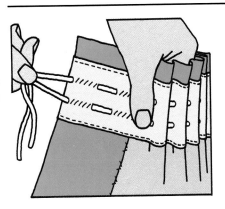

8 *Turn up bottom hem*
At bottom edge, turn 1cm to the wrong side and press. Turn balance of hem allowance to wrong side, pin and tack. Press complete curtain and hang on the track or pole for several days as fabric usually 'drops' slightly. Then adjust the hem if necessary and slipstitch into place.

Fabrics can be weighted to improve the way they hang by putting special lead weight tape in the hems.

DETACHABLE LININGS ADDED TO SIMPLE CURTAINS

Unless curtains are sheer, or specifically intended to filter light, it is usually best to line them. This protects the curtain fabric from the damaging effects of strong sunlight, and to some extent from outside dirt, as well as cutting out bright light and draughts from the windows.

A detachable lining is the simplest of all to make up and can easily be added to existing unlined curtains. Separate curtain linings are especially useful if curtain and lining have different launder-ing requirements – if one fabric is dry-cleanable only and the other washable, for example. The linings can be removed easily for frequent cleaning, and you can take them down during the warm summer months to create a lighter, airier atmosphere and to filter the sunlight.

Another plus for detachable linings is that they generally use less fabric than sewn-in linings since, whichever type of heading is on the curtain, you need only 1½ times the track width of fabric.

Lining fabric is generally cotton although, for a little extra cost, you can buy thermal curtain-lining fabric which provides better insulation. It is available in three colours, cream, black and silver.

Special heading tape for detachable linings is designed to be used with the hooks which are attached to the heading tape on the curtain. Some curtain track runners have a curtain hook combined with an additional ring for hooking on a lining.

---

1 *Make up the lining*
Measure up and cut out the lining fabric using the same method as for standard unlined curtain. Bear in mind, though, that the lining must be 2.5cm shorter than the curtain so that it will not show when the curtain is hung.

Join fabric widths as necessary and stitch side hems.

2 *Prepare the tape*
Lining heading tape is made up of two 'skirts', which fit over the top of the lining fabric like an envelope. The right side of the tape is the corded side.

Cut a length of heading tape to the width of the lining, plus at least 8cm for neatening the ends. At one end of the tape, pull the two cords free and secure with a knot. Trim off surplus tape up to the knot.

3 *Attach the tape* △
Ease the two skirts apart and slip the top of the lining between the skirts, with the corded side on the right side of the lining and the knotted end at the centre edge of the lining, overhanging by 1cm. Fold this short tape edge to form a 5mm double hem on the wrong side of the lining and stitch in place.

4 *Stitch the tape* △
At outer edge of the lining, pull 4cm of each cord free and trim surplus tape so that it overhangs lining by 1cm. Neaten the tape edge with a 5mm double hem on wrong side of lining, leaving the loose cords free for gathering up. Tack and machine tape in place, close to the bottom edge, stitching through both skirts of the tape and the curtain. Machine down both short sides, taking care not to stitch over the loose cords. Remove tacking.

5 *Gather the heading*
Pull the loose cords gently, pushing up the fabric and tape at the same time, until the fabric is the required fullness and width. Then knot the cords and tuck them out of sight.

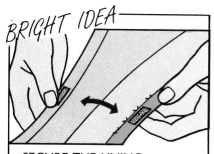

SECURE THE LINING
To hold a detachable lining in place and improve the hang of the curtains, stitch short strips of narrow Velcro to the side hems of linings and curtains at about 30cm intervals.

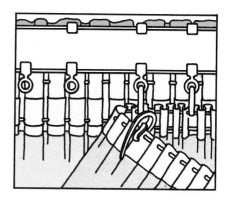

6 *Hang the curtains and linings* △
Insert hooks every 8cm along the top of the lining tape. With wrong side of lining and wrong side of curtain facing, fit the hooks through the slits on the curtain heading tape, so that both lining and curtain hang from the same hooks.

Combined hooks and runners △
If the curtain track has runners with combined hooks and rings, slot the hooks on the lining tape through the rings under the main curtain hooks.

CURTAINS WITH SEWN-IN LININGS

The sewn-in method of lining is suitable for most curtains and gives them a neat finish and a good hang.

A curtain lining acts as a barrier between the curtain and window and fulfils several functions. It cuts down light penetration, provides extra insulation, and protects the curtain fabric from the damaging effects of sunlight, and to some extent from dirt and dust. A lining also weighs down the curtain, giving it more body and a better hang.

There are several ways of lining curtains: the method you choose largely depends on the size and weight of the curtain – see below. This chapter covers making sewn-in linings. It also covers matching patterned fabrics, and adding a pleated frill to the edges of the curtain.

CHOOSING THE LINING METHOD

The method you choose depends on size of curtain, weight of fabric and, of course, personal preference.

A sewn-in lining is one of the easiest methods of lining curtains, and is ideal as long as the curtain fabric and lining can be laundered together. The lining is attached to the curtain across the top and sides, but left free at the hem for the best possible hang.

A locked-in lining is suitable for curtains that are very wide, or long and heavy or when an interlining is used. In addition to being attached across top and sides, the lining is invisibly lock-stitched to the curtain fabric at regular intervals over the whole curtain.

A detachable lining is ideal if curtain and lining fabrics have different laundering requirements, or if you want to add a lining to an existing unlined curtain – see opposite.

LINING FABRIC

Lining fabric is generally 100 per cent cotton, with a close weave to cut out light and draughts, and is available in a wide range of colours. Thermal curtain-lining fabric, with a special coating on one side, is a little more expensive but provides extra insulation. It is available in cream, black and silver.

Estimating fabric Calculate the amount of fabric needed for each curtain using the same method as for unlined curtains – see page 8.

Then work out what the curtains will measure when made up. The lining fabric should be the same length as the finished curtain, but 1cm less than the finished width of the curtain.

A neat finish

These full-length curtains benefit greatly from being lined. As well as cutting out bright light and draughts, a lining gives curtains more body so they hang better and it makes them look tidier from the outside of the window.

SEWN-IN LININGS

A sewn-in lining is the most common way to line curtains. With this method, curtain and lining are attached by being sewn together down the side hems and across the top while the hem of the lining is left hanging loose.

Before making up sewn-in linings, see Simple Unlined Curtains for basic curtain-making techniques.

1 Join fabric widths

Cut out curtain and lining fabric. If necessary, join fabric widths together to make up each curtain and lining, using 1.5cm flat seams as described for unlined curtains.

Flat fell seams or french seams are not necessary as the edges of the seam will be hidden between the lining and the curtain.

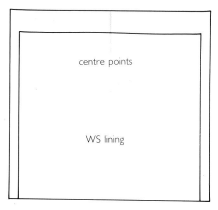

centre points

WS lining

2 Mark centre point on fabric △

Mark the centre point on the wrong side of both the curtain fabric and the lining fabric with tailor's chalk.

3 Pin lining and curtain fabric △

Position the lining on top of the curtain fabric, with right sides together and the top of the lining 4cm (if using standard curtain heading tape) below the top of the curtain fabric.

Match raw edges together down both sides, pin and tack. You will find that the curtain fabric is a little wider than the lining, so allow the curtain to form a few folds in order to match raw edges exactly.

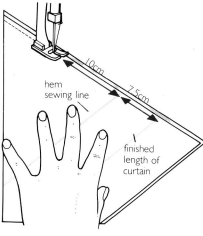

hem sewing line

10cm

7.5cm

finished length of curtain

4 Mark the curtain length △

Measuring from the top edge of the lining fabric (this will also be the top edge of the finished curtain, see Step 6), mark the curtain length required on to both lining and curtain fabric with tailor's chalk. Then mark the position of the hem sewing line for the curtain, allowing for a 7.5cm double hem.

Taking 1cm seams, stitch down both sides from the top of lining to within 10cm of the chalked hem sewing line.

5 Press curtain and lining △

Press the side seams open. Then turn the curtain and lining fabric through to the right side.

Carefully press the complete curtain, making sure that the chalk-marked centre points on the lining and curtain fabric (see Step 2) match up exactly, so that there is a 1.5cm margin of curtain fabric showing on each side of the lining.

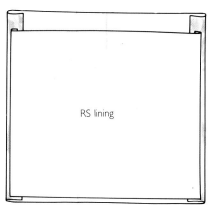

RS lining

6 Attach heading tape △

Fold top of curtain fabric to wrong side over top edge of lining, turning the corners in at a slight angle if necessary. Press and tack. Position heading tape over raw edge of curtain fabric, tack and stitch in place.

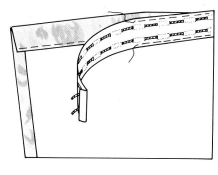

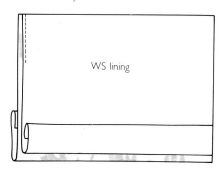

WS lining

7 Hem curtain and lining △

Turn curtain and lining through to the wrong side. Turn up a double hem 7.5cm deep along the bottom of the curtain fabric, with mock mitres at corners (opposite). Pin and tack.

Turn up a double hem to wrong side of lining fabric, so that lining hangs about 2cm above bottom edge of curtain. Make the lining hem the same as, or just less than, the depth of the curtain hem, trimming off surplus fabric if necessary. Pin and tack in place.

8 Pull up heading tape

Turn curtain right side out again and press. Pull up heading tape to make the curtain the right width for the window, and hang in place for several days to give the fabric time to 'drop'. Then adjust hems if necessary, and slipstitch in place. If the hang of the curtain needs to be improved, enclose curtain weights in the hem of the curtain before stitching it down.

Finish by slipstitching the lower side edges of lining to the curtain.

MOCK MITRES

Mitring is the neatest way of finishing corners of hems. A true mitre should be at a 45° angle. On curtains, however, the bottom hem is deeper than the side hems and a 'mock' mitre is the simplest method. To make a mock mitred corner, only one side of the corner (the bottom hem) is mitred, and not at a 45° angle.

With sewn-in linings, the lining and curtain fabric are sewn together to within 10cm of the curtain's hem sewing line – see Step 4.

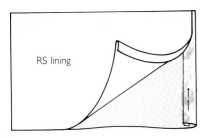

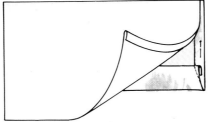

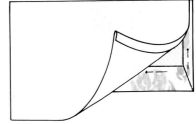

☐ Turn in and press the remaining side seam allowance along each side of curtain.

☐ Turn up and press a double 7.5cm deep hem along the bottom of the curtain fabric.

☐ Fold corner of hem in at an angle until top of diagonal touches top of side hem.

MATCHING PATTERNS

Unless windows are very narrow, a curtain will probably be made up of more than one width of fabric. If you are using fabric with a bold pattern, the pattern must match horizontally at seams and at the leading edges (where a pair of curtains join when closed). To do this, you must allow extra fabric so that 'pattern repeats' can be adjusted to match up.

Pattern repeats The pattern repeat is often quoted on fabric details. If not, measure the depth of the pattern repeat along the selvedge edge of the fabric between the top of one pattern and the top of the next pattern down. Then add one pattern repeat for each fabric width required.

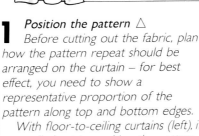

1 *Position the pattern △*
Before cutting out the fabric, plan how the pattern repeat should be arranged on the curtain – for best effect, you need to show a representative proportion of the pattern along top and bottom edges.

With floor-to-ceiling curtains (left), it's generally best to position the pattern repeat so that it starts near the top turning of the curtain.

With short sill-length curtains (right), the lower edge is nearest eye level and it's best to position the pattern repeat so that it ends near the bottom hemline. You'll find that a half pattern at the top of the curtain is more easily absorbed in the heading.

2 *Start cutting out fabric*
Cut the first piece of fabric to the required length (drop of curtain plus top and bottom hem allowances).

Make sure you cut perfectly straight across the width. If the fabric has a straight thread pattern, pull out a thread which runs across the width and cut along the gap. Otherwise, mark a straight cutting line at right angles to the selvedges with tailor's chalk and a straight edge.

3 *Match the pattern △*
Lay the first piece of fabric out flat, right side up. Then lay the rest of the fabric out alongside, right side up, and match the pattern horizontally with the first cut piece.

Cut the second piece of fabric so it starts and ends at exactly the same point of the pattern as the first piece. Continue in this way until you have cut all the required number of fabric widths.

4 *Join fabric widths*
Mark with a pin the centre of each pattern repeat along the side edges of the two fabric widths that are to be joined. Using a flat seam, lay the two pieces of fabric together with right sides facing, and the edges and pins matching. Then pin along the seamline 1.5cm from the edges.

Turn the fabric to the right side, check that the pattern is matching exactly along the seam, and make adjustments if necessary. Tack along the seamline, remove pins and stitch seam. Remove tacking and press seam open.

BRIGHT IDEA

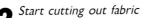

COLOURED LINING

Use pastel-coloured lining to alter the tone of light that comes through pale curtains – soft pink or peach can dramatically warm up cold winter light. Make sure that the lining colour complements that of the curtain by holding the fabrics up to the light together.

ADDING A PLEATED FRILL

A pleated frill along bottom and leading (or closing) edges of a curtain looks crisp and smart. For a neat trim at seams between frill and curtain, use piping cord covered with a toning coloured fabric.

Measuring up Cut curtain lining to the same size as curtain fabric, and join fabric widths as necessary to make up each curtain and lining.

To calculate the amount of fabric needed for a double-sided pleated frill, double the finished frill width (say, 6cm) and add a 3cm allowance (to give a total width of 15cm). If you have a ruffler attachment for your sewing machine, you can use this to make single-sided pleats quickly; in this case, neaten the lower long edge of frill with a double 10mm hem.

For the length of the frill, measure leading and bottom edges of curtain. Multiply this measurement by three and add a 3cm seam allowance, plus additional seam allowances if joining strips of fabric to make up the length. Then allow for an extra pleat to help ease the frill round the bottom corner. To do this, decide on the pleat width (the part visible when the pleat is stitched in place – usually between 12mm and 3cm wide), and multiply by three.

1 *Fold fabric in half*
If necessary, join strips of fabric together with flat seams pressed open. Fold the frill fabric in half along its length with right sides together, and stitch across each end with 1.5cm seams. Then turn fabric to the right side – wrong sides together, raw edges matching – and press.

2 *Make up pleats*
To get the number of pleats, divide the length of the edge to be frilled by the pleat width. Then add on one pleat (the extra allowed for the corner).

Lay the frill fabric flat, and use tailor's chalk to mark the width of the pleat (A-B, B-C and so on) along the fabric at right angles to the frill edge. Then fold and pin A to C, and repeat until you reach the end of the frill. Tack along top and bottom of the pleats to hold them in place and press.

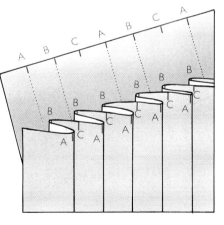

3 △ *Sew piping to curtain*
Make up the piping. Then use tailor's chalk to mark a 1.5cm seam allowance on the right side of curtain along closing and bottom edges. Pin and tack piping along this chalk line: at the bottom corner, snip into the piping fabric up to the stitching and ease it round in a slight curve.

To finish, trim the piping cord level with what will be the edge of the finished curtain. Trim the fabric covering the cord to within 1cm of edge and tuck inside to neaten.

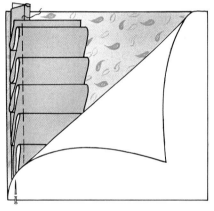

4 *Sew frill to curtain fabric* △
Place the frill over the piping on the right side of the curtain, with raw edges matching; pin and tack in place.

Then lay the lining fabric on top of the curtain fabric (so that the frill and piping are sandwiched in between at bottom and closing edges), with right sides facing and raw edges matching. Pin, tack and stitch in place. Trim, then press seams and turn curtain through to the right side.

5 *Complete the curtain*
Pin the top edges of the lining and the curtain fabric together. Fold the top of the curtain and lining fabric to the wrong side, press and tack in place. Position heading tape to cover the raw edge of the curtain fabric. Pin, tack and stitch in place leaving the frill and piping free. Then press the complete curtain.

Finally, pull up the heading tape so that the curtain fits the window, tie cords together and tuck them out of sight. Insert hooks and hang the curtain.

LACE AND SHEER CURTAINS

Net curtains can be merely functional, affording a measure of privacy, or they can add an extra decorative touch.

Sheer curtains are traditionally hung at windows to give privacy to a room which is overlooked, or to screen an unsightly view. Since they become transparent at night, when the light is on in the room, it is also necessary to hang additional curtains – or fit blinds – for privacy at night. However, in some situations, sheer or lace curtains are hung purely for decorative effect, adding a feminine touch to a room. In such situations it may not be necessary to hang any extra curtains, although they are often a practical addition, helping to cut down on heat loss at night. Roman, austrian, festoon or roller blinds may provide alternative screening at night.

NET EFFECTS

The simplest effect with sheer curtains is a plain, translucent drop of white or off-white cotton or synthetic fabric. Such curtains are usually hung from a lightweight track, using a slightly transparent heading tape specially designed for use with sheer fabrics. You can also hang the curtains from an expanding curtain wire or lightweight rod (such as a café rod), slotted through a casing in the top of the curtain.

There are innumerable other effects you can achieve: there are specially designed ready-made net curtains in crossover or jardinière styles, for example. You can also create tiered effects with café curtains, tied-back curtains and valances all in net fabrics. Or if you only want to do a minimum of sewing you can simply drape panels of lace or voile over a wooden curtain pole.

If the sheer curtains are to be fitted to a pivot window or a glazed door, you can stop the fabric from flapping and getting trapped in the window or door by making a casing at both the top and the bottom of the curtain and slotting both casings on to wires or rods.

BUYING FABRIC FOR SHEERS

There is a wide range of sheer fabrics to choose from if you are planning to make net curtains.

Many manufacturers produce sheer plain or patterned fabric by the metre, in the same standard widths as ordinary curtain fabric, as well as wider widths for larger windows. You can also buy panels of lace in various sizes ready to make up into curtains. These panels usually have a pattern designed to suit the size of the panel, often with scalloped edges. They sometimes have slots or eyelets at the top, so that you don't need to do any sewing at all. You just thread them straight on to a curtain rod.

Another alternative is to buy special sheer curtain fabric which is made with a casing along one edge and a scalloped or hemmed finish along the opposite edge. This type of fabric is used sideways, so that the width of the fabric you buy becomes the drop of the curtain. When you buy it by the metre, the length should be about one and a half times the finished width of the curtain. All you have to do is hem the ends to form the sides of the curtain. If you are buying this type of sheer curtain it is advisable to check on the different widths available before you fit the curtain rod.

Layered look
A single café curtain screens the lower half of this window, while a pair of curtains with a matching heading add a decorative touch. Both tiers are hung from rings on substantial brass poles set inside the recess.

SPECIAL SEWING TECHNIQUES

Because of the nature of sheer fabrics, there are one or two points to bear in mind when working with them.

Seams are unsightly in sheer fabric. Where possible, avoid them altogether: simply make up two or three curtains to fit the window, and arrange them so that the gathers hide the edges of the fabric. If you do have to join widths of fabric (when making a long frill to edge a curtain, for example) use french seams, which are stitched so that the raw edges are neatly tucked inside the structure of the seam.

Hems should be double (1cm double hems down side edges, 4cm double hems across lower edges of curtains). It is essential that raw edges are cut straight and even, as you will be able to see them inside the hems.

If the fabric is synthetic, you will have to take extra care when pressing it: use a very cool iron. After washing sheer synthetic curtains, it is advisable to hang them *in situ* to dry, so that the creases fall out as much as possible to save unnecessary pressing.

Always use a sharp, fine needle and a fairly long, loose stitch. Choose a fine thread, and use polyester thread for synthetic fabrics and cotton for cotton sheers.

FRENCH SEAMS

Avoid seams in sheer fabrics where possible. If necessary, use french seams to join widths of fabric. Allow 2cm seam allowance for seams made by this method.

1 *Join the widths* ▷
The first step is to join the two widths of fabric, wrong sides facing and raw edges matching, taking a 1cm seam. Trim a couple of millimetres from the raw edges for a neat edge.

2 *Turn and neaten* ▷
The second row of stitching forms the actual seamline, and encloses the raw edges at the same time: turn the fabric back on itself so that the right sides are facing and the seam allowance is enclosed between the layers of fabric. With right sides facing, pin, tack and stitch, positioning the seamline 1cm in from the previous row of stitching. When you look at the seam from the right side of the fabric, there are no obvious stitching lines.

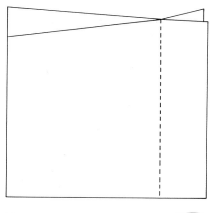
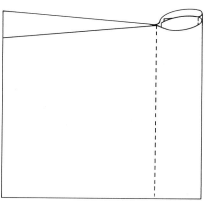

CHECK YOUR NEEDS

☐ Appropriate hardware – curtain track, rod, pole, or expanding curtain wire – with hooks, runners or rings as necessary
☐ Lace or sheer fabric
☐ Sharp cutting-out scissors
☐ Tape measure
☐ Heading tape (unless made up with a casing)
☐ Pins, needles, and thread
☐ Sewing machine
☐ Contrast fabric for trimming (fine cotton or lace – optional)

CURTAINS WITH HEADING

Lace or plain sheer curtains with a heading formed by a specially-designed tape are made in the same way as unlined curtains. You have to take extra care to ensure the stitching is straight and even, since the transparent nature of the fabric means that any faults on the wrong side will show on the right side.

1 *Measure up*
Fit the curtain track or pole in place at the top of the window, or half-way up for café curtains. Measure the length of the pole and the drop of the curtains. In most cases, you will make a single curtain to screen the whole window, unless you want to be able to draw the curtains back for any reason.

2 *Calculate fabric quantities*
The length of fabric required is equal to the length of the finished curtain, plus 3cm for the heading and 8cm for the hem. The width is 1½-2 times the width of the finished curtain (the length of the curtain track). If you need to join widths of fabric, check whether you need to include an allowance for pattern matching.

3 *Prepare the fabric*
Check that the fabric has been cut squarely across the lower edge. (You can use the edge of a rectangular table to check this: lay the fabric out so the sides are parallel to the sides of the table, and check that the ends run parallel to the ends of the table.)

4 *Side hems* ▷
Turn under a 1cm double hem down each side edge, and pin, tack and stitch in place. If the selvedge is not too tightly woven, take a single, 1cm hem.

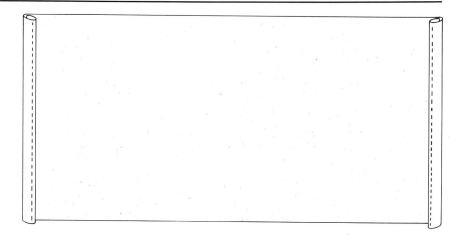

5 Lower hem ▷

Turn under 4cm across the lower edge, and then a further 4cm. Pin, tack and stitch in place, using a machine straight stitch. (On heavier, patterned cotton lace you may prefer to use a hand slipstitch.)

Cut the heading tape to the same width as the curtain, plus 4cm. Turn under 2cm at each end of the tape, pull out the cords and knot them together.

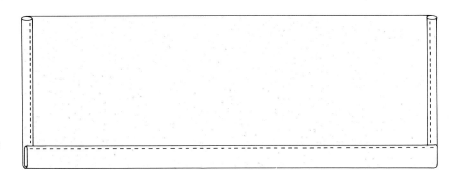

6 Heading ▷

Turn under 3cm across the top of the curtain, turn under the corners and press. Pin the tape to the wrong side of the top of the curtain, a couple of millimetres below the fold line so that the raw edge is covered. Tack and stitch in place a couple of millimetres in from the edge of the tape. Draw up the fullness so the curtain is the same width as the track and hang in place.

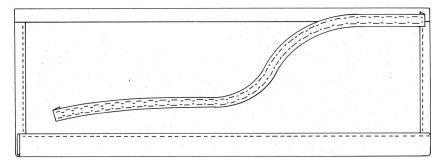

FRILLED CURTAINS

These curtains are made up in plain Terylene sheer fabric, with a cased heading. A 6cm-deep frill in a fine (non-sheer) patterned fabric stands out around each curtain. In the instructions given here the edge of the frill has been hemmed. Alternatively, you could bind the edges, or neaten them with a closed-up satin stitch (in which case you can omit the hem allowance along one edge of the frill).

The curtains are made up as a pair; for extra effect you could arrange them so that they overlap, joining them together at the top before adding the casing.

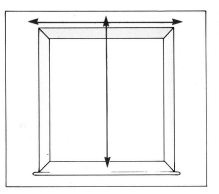
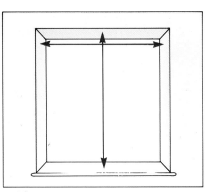

1 Measure up △

Decide on the position of the curtain rod: for this style it is better to fit the rod on the outside of the recess. If it is fitted inside the recess it should be 6cm down from the top of the reveal, to allow room for the frill to stand at the top of the curtains. (If the rod is inside the recess you should also allow 6cm for the frill on either side.) Measure the length of the rod and the finished overall drop of the curtains (including the frills all round).

2 Calculate sheer fabric

Divide the length of the curtain rod by two. For the plain part of each curtain you need a panel of fabric 1½-2 times this measurement, depending on the fullness required. The panel should be the length of the finished curtain, less a total of 10cm to allow for the frill and a 1cm turning top and bottom. You will also need a strip of fabric 4cm wide to form a casing across the back of the curtain.

3 Calculate fabric for frill

The length of the frill for each curtain is 1½ times the total perimeter of the panel calculated in Step 2 (2 × length + 2 × width). The depth is 6cm plus 3cm hem and seam allowance.

4 Make up the frill ▷

Join lengths of fabric to form a frill 1½ times the perimeter of the plain panel. Join the ends of the frill to form a complete ring. Use french seams for a neat finish. Turn under and stitch a 1cm double hem along the long, outer edge of the frill. Pin, tack and stitch in place, then press. Alternatively, omit seam allowance and bind edge of frill or use a closed up zigzag stitch for a neat finish.

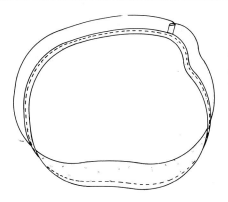

5 Gather the frill

Divide and mark the frill into four equal sections. Make two rows of gathering stitch along the unfinished edge, 1cm from the raw edge.

6 *Attach the frill* ▷
Mark the centre of each edge of the panel. Draw up frill so that it is the same length as the perimeter of the panel. Pin the frill to the panel right sides facing and raw edges matching. Distribute the fullness evenly, and match the marks on the frill to the marks on the panel, allowing a little extra fullness at corners. Tack in place. With the right side of the curtain facing you, stitch through both layers of fabric, taking 1cm seams. Remove gathering and tacking stitches and neaten raw edges together with zigzag stitch. Carefully press the seam allowances towards the frill.

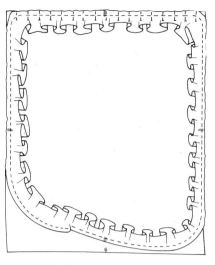

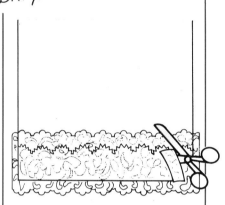

7 *Prepare strip for casing* △
Cut a 4cm-wide strip of fabric half the length of the rod. Turn under and tack a 1cm hem down each long edge.

8 *Gather heading*
Run two lines of gathering stitch across the top of the panel, one line just inside the seamline, and the other 17mm below that. Draw up gathering threads so that the width of each curtain is approximately the same length as the prepared casing.

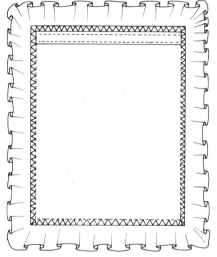

9 *Attach casing* ◁
Lay the frilled panel out, wrong side up. Pin the casing to the panel so that the top of the casing matches the seamline. (Note that the casing should match the plain panel, and not overlap the frill.) If the curtains are hung in a recess, you should make the strip for the casing slightly shorter than half the width of the curtain rod. Tack the casing in place along upper and lower edges. Stitch the casing to the curtain 2mm from each long folded edge of the casing. Make up the second curtain in exactly the same way. Slot the curtains on to the rod. If they tend to pull apart, stitch the corners together.

BRIGHT IDEA

ADDING A TRIM

If you do not like the designs of lace-trimmed sheer fabrics that are available ready-made, you can add your own trim. Buy a piece of plain sheer fabric 1½-2 times the width of the window and slightly longer than the finished length you require. Buy a strip of trimming the same width as the sheer fabric. Lay the lace over the lower edge of the curtain, wrong side of trim facing right side of curtain, so that the lower edge of the trim is level with the unfinished edge of the curtain. Pin and tack in place. Zigzag stitch the lace to the sheer fabric, about 1cm from the top edge of the trim, following the shape of the trim if appropriate. Turn over and trim away the raw edge of the sheer fabric close to the zigzag stitching before making up.

◁ **Frilled to perfection**
Panels of plain sheer Terylene fabric have been finished with frills to match the bed linen in this teenage bedroom. The heading is a simple casing, which slips on to a curtain rod fitted across the top of the recess.

CAFE CURTAINS

Traditionally used in French cafés to screen the lower half of the window, these curtains are economical to make.

Café curtains are a practical alternative to net curtains, to screen part of the window during the day where you want to maintain privacy without blocking out all the light, or where you want to hide an unsightly view. They hang from a pole, rod, or curtain wire fixed halfway up the window, and are not usually as tightly gathered as normal curtains. There is usually only a single curtain at each window, rather than a pair. They can be left unlined, both to let in as much light as possible and for economy.

CHOOSE YOUR FABRICS
Café curtains look particularly good in crisp cotton furnishing fabrics. Choose fabrics which are fast dyed, as they are likely to be exposed to sunlight for a fair proportion of the day.

Another point to bear in mind is that the curtains will be seen from outside the window. Colour-woven patterns, such as gingham, might be an appropriate choice if you are worried about how the curtains look from outside.

Otherwise, you can line the curtains in much the same way as standard curtains using plain lining or self fabric (see Curtains with Sewn-in Linings).

STYLES OF HEADING
There is a wide choice of different headings suitable for café curtains.
Casings A simple casing can be made at the top of the curtain by making two parallel rows of stitching and slipping the curtain on to a curtain rod (or expanding curtain wire).
Curtain tapes You can use any of the light- or medium-weight curtain heading tapes, and then hang the curtains from rings on a rod or pole. Special café rods are available for this purpose.
Simple scalloped heading One of the most traditional styles for these curtains is to cut semi-circular scoops out of the top of the curtain, neatening them with binding or a facing, and stitching a ring between each of the scallops. The ring then slips on to a purpose-designed 'café rod' (usually brass), or a lightweight

wooden curtain pole.
Looped and scalloped heading Another alternative is to hang the curtain from a pole by loops made by cutting deep scallops out of the top of the curtain. The strips between the scallops are extended so that they can be stitched to the back of the curtain to form the loops which are slotted on to the pole. Alternatively, cut out deep rectangles, rather than scallops, for a castellated effect at the heading.
Scallops and pleats A more sophisticated variation of this is to combine scallops with hand-made triple pleats. Cut scallops as before, but leave a wider strip between them so that you can make pleats by hand, and hang the curtain by rings from a pole. For a neat finish, the curtains should be lined, or the scalloped shapes faced with matching fabric.

FINISHING TOUCHES
Frills in either matching or contrasting fabric are an appropriate optional extra for café curtains.

You should also think about how to dress the rest of the window. Instead of ordinary curtains or a blind to draw at night, you could add a pair of short curtains, made in the same way as the café curtain. Hang them from a rod at the top of the window, so that they close above the café curtains.

A valance at the top, made to match the curtain, helps to frame the window if you don't want to screen it completely at night. Another idea is to make simple swags and tails to give the window a dressier look.

MEASURING UP
Measure the window where the café curtain is to hang: usually the track is positioned halfway down the window, but you may want to adjust this slightly to suit the window.

Once you have fixed the rod in place, measure the finished width and length of the curtain. For a plain scalloped heading you will need a piece of fabric slightly wider than the window; for a pleated scalloped heading you will need a piece of fabric nearly twice the width of the window, and for a cased heading you will need enough fabric to make up a panel one and a half times the finished width. Add an allowance for side hems, headings and hems.

Country style
Bring a breath of fresh air to a kitchen or bathroom – here a scalloped heading has been made, and fitted on a white, fluted café pole.

CHECK YOUR NEEDS

☐ Curtain fabric
☐ Interfacing (optional, for scalloped headings)
☐ Lining (optional)
☐ Curtain pole or rod
☐ Curtain rings (for scalloped headings)
☐ Sewing thread
☐ Needles and pins
☐ Sewing machine
☐ Paper for pattern (for scalloped headings)

PLAIN, SCALLOPED CURTAIN

The simplest scalloped curtains have curtain rings stitched or clipped to the strip between each scallop. They are unpleated, and should be made slightly wider than the window. To ensure a neat finish, the top is faced. The instructions here include interfacing for a crisp look.

1 Measure up
Start by fitting the pole across the window at an appropriate height. Measure the distance from the pole to the sill, and the width of the window.

2 Calculate fabric amounts
The width of the curtain is equal to the width of the window, plus 3cm seam allowance, and an extra allowance of about 10cm to allow the curtain to hang in very gentle folds. The length is equal to the measured length, plus 10cm to make a turned-under facing. The top of the curtain will hang about 1cm beneath the pole, so taking this into account, you need allow only 3cm for a 2cm double hem along the lower edge.

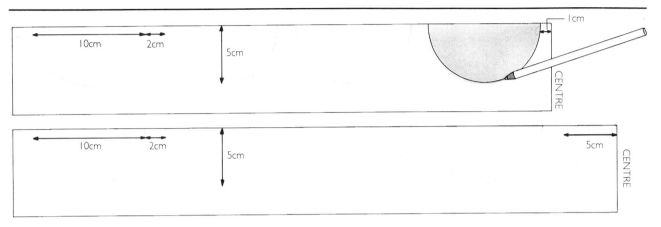

3 Make a pattern △
Use a strip of paper 9cm deep and half the width of the finished curtain to make a pattern to ensure the scallops are evenly shaped and spaced. One end of the paper will be positioned at the centre of the curtain, and the other at the outer edge.

Semi-circular scallops create a pleasing effect, so use compasses or a suitable saucer to draw them. Good dimensions for the scallops are about 5cm deep, 10cm wide and 2cm apart. They will be easier to draw if you first cut out a card template. Position the scallops so that either one is in the

centre of the curtain, or there is a space between the scallops at the centre (in this case, allow 1cm, as the pattern is placed on a fold). Adjust the size and spacings of the scallops and the width of the curtain until they fit neatly across the width. Cut out the scallop shapes.

4 Cut out fabric
Adjust the calculations made in step 2 to accommodate an exact number of scallops if necessary, including the appropriate turning allowance down each side. Cut out the fabric to this measurement. Turn under and press

10cm along the top edge. Cut a strip of iron-on interfacing 9cm deep, and the same width as the finished curtain, to interface the top edge of the curtain.

5 Interface the top edge
Position the interfacing on the wrong side of the curtain, 1.5cm in from each side edge and 1cm from the top edge, so that the lower edge of the interfacing matches the fold line at the top of the curtain. Press in place.

6 Neaten edges △
Turn under and stitch 1cm along top edge of curtain, over interfacing. Turn under 5mm and then a further 1cm down each side edge.

7 Mark scallops △
Turn the interfaced section over to the right side, turning back along fold line and pin in place. Mark the centre of the curtain. Position centre edge of pattern on centre mark and pin in place. Draw round the curves of the scallops. Remove the pattern and repeat for opposite half of curtain.

8 Cut out and stitch △
Cut out the scallop shapes along the top folded edge, cutting 1cm outside marked lines to allow for a seam. Machine stitch along each of the marked lines to create a series of scallops. Notch seam allowances. Trim and layer seam allowances. Press, turn right side out and press again.

9 Finish edges and attach rings
Slipstitch neatened edges of curtain and facing together at each end of the heading.

10 Turn up hem
Turn up and stitch a 2cm double hem by hand or machine, mitring corners neatly.

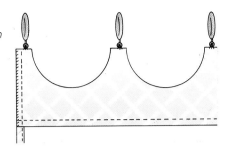

11 Attach rings ◁
Stitch a curtain ring to the top of each scallop by hand, and thread the curtain on to the pole.

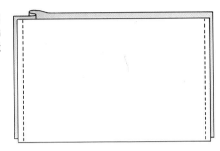

TRIPLE-PLEATED SCALLOPS

Adding pleats to the curtain heading creates a fuller, more sophisticated effect. They are made in much the same way as unpleated café curtains, but you have to allow an extra 12cm between the scallops, so that you can create a set of three 1.5cm deep pleats.

1 Make a pattern
Start by making a pattern the finished width of the curtain, as for the plain scalloped heading opposite. Cut down halfway between each scallop. Space the scallops an extra 12cm apart, so there is a 14cm space between scallops. Pin them on to another strip of paper and draw round them, to create a wider pattern. You will now have a pattern for half the curtain.

2 Calculate fabric amounts
The width of fabric is twice the width of the pattern, plus 5cm seam allowance at the sides. The depth is the same as the distance from the pole to the sill. No seam allowance is needed at the top, since the top of the curtain hangs about a centimetre below the pole. Add 5cm hem allowance. The lining should be the same depth but 2cm narrower.

3 Make up curtain △
Place lining on fabric, right sides together and raw edges matching across top and bottom. Pin together down side edges, raw edges matching. Stitch down sides, taking 1.5cm seam.

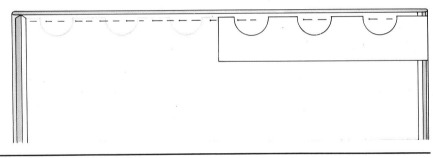

4 Make scalloped heading ▷
Press lightly so that lining is central to curtain (with a 1cm border down each side). Trim seam allowances and press open. Pin lining to curtain across top. Position pattern across top of curtain, 1cm from top edge. Mark curves on to lining, first on one half, then on the other.

5 Interface heading
Cut a strip of iron-on interfacing the same width as the finished curtain, and 10cm deep. Position on wrong side of curtain, level with top edge. Iron in place.

6 Cut out and stitch scallops ▷
Cut out marked scallops through both layers of fabric and interfacing leaving a 1cm seam allowance. Pin, tack and stitch along upper edge of curtain, between and around scallops, taking a 1cm seam allowance. Notch curves. Turn right side out and press.

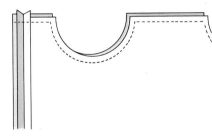

7 Make pinch pleats ▷
For each pinch pleat, fold the section to be pleated in half, wrong sides facing. Make a line of stitching by hand or machine 4.5cm from fold line (i.e. 1cm from the edge of the scallop). The stitching should extend 10cm down the curtain from the top edge. Open out fabric and lay it so that the stitched fold sticks up and the stitching is flat against the surface. With one finger on either side of the pleat, open the pleat out, pinch the centre fold, and push it down towards the line of stitching to form a triple pleat. Grip the pleats in place and smooth them so that the folds are even. Pin in place.

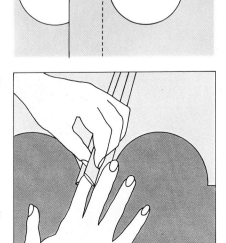

8 Stitch the pleats △
With the inner folds firmly pinned so they are as close to the vertical line of stitching as possible, stitch across the pleat, level with the bottom of the vertical line of stitching, using a fine stab stitch. At the top of the pleat, catch the inner folds in place.

9 *Turn up hems*
Turn up hems on curtain and lining and stitch by hand.

10 *Attach fixing hooks*
Attach special pinch pleat hooks (with spikes) to each pleat, ready to hook on to the curtain rings.

CASED HEADING AND FRILL
Two lines of stitching across the top of the curtain make a casing with a crisp, upright stand at the top. It is a quick and easy method of heading a curtain, economical on both time and fabric. A frill along the lower edge softens the effect.

1 *Measure up*
To find the finished size of the single café curtain, measure from the top of the café rod or pole to the sill, and measure the length of the track (the width of the window).

2 *Calculate fabric amounts*
The length of the fabric panel for the curtain is equal to the measurement from the top of the pole to the sill, less 7cm (for an 8.5cm deep frill), plus 8cm to make the cased heading and allow a little extra fabric so the curtain will slot on to the pole easily. The width should be about one and a half times the length of the curtain pole. You also need a strip of fabric 11.5cm wide and three times the length of the curtain track to make the frill across the lower edge.

3 *Cut out fabric*
Cut out pieces of fabric to make up the panel for the curtain and the strip for the frill. Remember to allow 1.5cm for seams if you need to join widths of fabric. Join fabric widths if necessary.

4 *Make up frill*
Turn under 5mm and then a further 1cm along the lower edge and ends of the strip for the frill. Run two rows of gathering stitches along the upper edge.

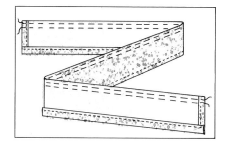

5 *Attach frill*
Draw up gathering threads so that frill is 3cm shorter than the lower edge of curtain. Pin and tack in place, right sides together and raw edges matching. Stitch, taking 1.5cm seams. To neaten raw edges, trim and zigzag stitch raw edges together and press seam upwards.

6 *Neaten raw edges*
Turn under 5mm and then a further 1cm down each side edge of the curtain. Pin, tack and stitch in place.

7 *Make casing along top edge* ▷
Turn under 1.5cm and then a further 6cm along top edge of curtain. Make two lines of stitching 1cm from each folded edge, to make a casing 4cm wide (to fit a pole up to 25mm diameter).

8 *Fit the curtain*
Slot the curtain on to the café rod, sliding it along the pole so that the fullness is evenly distributed.

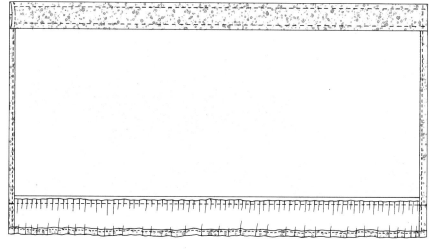

▷ *Frilled finish*
A crisp, unlined café curtain on a brass pole hides an unsightly view without cutting out too much light. A simple frill along the lower edge adds extra interest.

TRADITIONAL FABRIC PELMETS

A fabric pelmet is quite simple to make, and adds a decorative and distinctive finish to a window.

A pelmet is mainly used to add a decorative finish to the top of curtains, but it also conceals the curtain track and heading and helps to balance the proportions of a window. It can, for example, be fixed higher than the curtain track to make a window appear taller, or be extended at the sides to make it appear wider. Pelmets are also an effective link between curtains on adjoining sets of windows.

A traditional fabric pelmet is made of stiffened fabric that is attached to a pelmet board fitted across the top of the window. The board is a semi-permanent fixture once screwed into place, but the pelmet itself should be easy to remove for cleaning and is best attached with a touch-and-close fastener such as Velcro. Stiffened fabric is not washable, but it can easily be brushed and sponged with weak detergent or spray-on, brush-off dry cleaner.

The simplest pelmet is a straight rectangular one, or the bottom edge of the pelmet can be shaped for added interest. It can be made from the same fabric as the curtains, or from a contrasting or co-ordinating fabric.

Choosing fabric Almost any furnishing fabric, except very open weaves and sheers, can be used to cover a pelmet.

Before calculating how much fabric you need, fix the curtain track and pelmet board so that exact measurements can be taken – see overleaf.

CHOOSING A STYLE

Pelmets can be pretty and decorative, classic and elegant, or plain and simple. The style and shape that you choose depends on the style and size of the window and curtains, and the overall decor of the room. It also depends on the fabric being used for the curtains and pelmet, as certain fabric designs suit particular pelmet shapes better than others – stripes and geometrics, for example, go best with castellations, while florals combine well with pretty scalloped edges.

Draw up your own design, perhaps following one of the shapes illustrated here, or use a self-adhesive stiffening material that has various pelmet shapes printed on the backing paper.

Decorative shapes
△ *Good shapes for pelmets include soft scallops, castellations and zigzags.*
◁ *This attractive step-shaped pelmet, covered in a pretty floral chintz to match the curtains, adds interest to a rather plain window.*

TYPES OF FABRIC STIFFENER

The material traditionally used to stiffen fabric pelmets is buckram. More modern self-adhesive stiffener costs a little more, but is easy to use and ideal if you want to use a ready-printed design for the pelmet edge. Both can be bought from furnishing fabric departments.

Buckram is an open weave fabric that has been treated to make it stiff. Iron-on buckram is also available.

Making a pelmet with buckram involves quite a lot of hand sewing which takes time but gives a very professional finish. The pelmet fabric covering the buckram also needs to be backed with bump interlining or iron-on interfacing for a smooth finish.

Self-adhesive stiffeners have a peel-off backing paper printed with several pelmet styles, as well as a grid to simplify drawing your own design.

There are two main types of self-adhesive stiffener – single-sided and double-sided. With the single-sided type, the front is self-adhesive and the back is coated in a velour-style finish that makes lining unnecessary. Double-sided stiffener – with adhesive on both sides – does need lining but gives a neater finish. Both come in 30cm and 40cm widths; double-sided is also available in a 60cm width.

CHECK YOUR NEEDS
For the pelmet board:
☐ Plywood, 12mm thick
☐ Steel rule
☐ Saw
☐ Nails
☐ Hammer
☐ Brackets
☐ Drill and bit
☐ Screws
☐ Screwdriver

For the pelmet:
☐ Fabric
☐ Buckram or self-adhesive fabric stiffener
☐ Lining material (unless using single-sided self-adhesive stiffener)
☐ Interlining or iron-on interfacing (if using buckram)
☐ Tape measure
☐ Paper to make a template
☐ Scissors
☐ Sewing thread
☐ Pins, needles
☐ Sewing machine
☐ Iron and ironing board
☐ Velcro fastening
☐ Decorative braid plus fabric adhesive (optional)

A pelmet shelf ▽

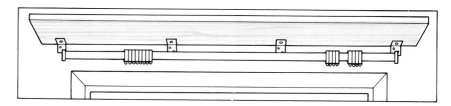

A pelmet box ▽

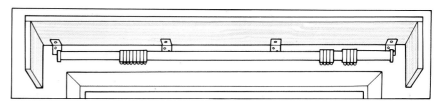

FITTING THE PELMET BOARD
The pelmet board may be constructed in various ways, depending on the shape and size of the window. It is made from 12mm thick plywood.

For most windows, a pelmet shelf (above, top) is adequate. This should be about 10cm deep to leave sufficient clearance for the bulk of the curtains when pulled back, and the same length as the curtain track plus about 12cm to give 6cm clearance on either side.

If the pelmet is particularly wide or deep, a pelmet box (above, bottom) with rectangular end pieces gives the fabric extra rigidity. In this case, nail a 10cm square piece of plywood at right angles to each end of the pelmet shelf.

To fix a shelf or box, position it centrally just above the curtain track and/or window frame, at the height where you want the top of the pelmet to come. Then fix it to the wall with small brackets spaced evenly along the board at approximately 20cm intervals. If there isn't sufficient space above the window for the fixings, you may be able to fit the board by screwing the brackets to the outer side edges of the window frame.

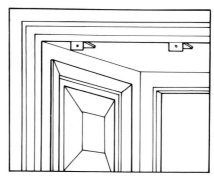 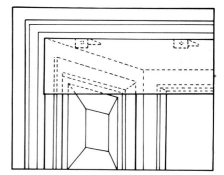

Recessed windows △
On deeply recessed windows (above, left and right), the pelmet board can be cut to the exact width of the recess and *fitted across the front of the window area, flush with the recess, with the fixing brackets screwed to the upper surface of the recess.*

HANGING THE PELMET
The simplest method of hanging a pelmet so that it can be removed easily – for cleaning, say – is to glue the hooked half of a strip of Velcro to the edges of the pelmet board. (The other half of the Velcro is stitched to the wrong side of the pelmet when making it up.) Alternatively, you can sew small brass rings to the back of the pelmet, and hook these over nails or screws fixed to the edge of the pelmet board.

A third method is to tack the pelmet to the board with upholstery tacks and cover the tacks with braid glued in place with fabric adhesive, but this has to be dismantled every time you take the pelmet down for cleaning.

MEASURING UP
Measure along the front of the pelmet board, and round the short side ends if you're using a pelmet box. This gives the finished length of the pelmet.

Having chosen a suitable shape for the pelmet edge, the depth of the pelmet depends largely on the size of the curtains, but 15-30cm is about average.

MAKING A TEMPLATE

If you're making a pelmet to your own design, you need to make a template from which to cut the pelmet shape. (If you're using self-adhesive stiffener, you can of course draw the shape directly on to the backing paper grid.)

1 Draw the shaped edge
Cut a strip of paper slightly longer than the finished length of the pelmet and slightly wider than the deepest section of the planned shape. Fold the paper in half widthways, and mark the position of the side edges, if any, with a crease. Then draw half of the pelmet shape you want on to the folded paper – working from centre out to edges.

2 Cut out the shape
Cut out the shape from the folded paper, and trim the top edge if necessary to make the template fit the pelmet board exactly. Unfold the paper and check its proportions against the window before cutting out the fabric.

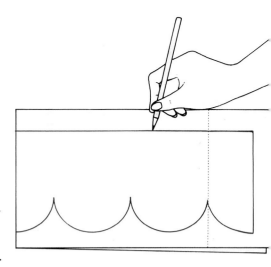

CUTTING OUT

To make up the pelmet, you need to cut out the following:

☐ **Fabric stiffener** Cut a piece of buckram or self-adhesive stiffener to the finished shape and size of pelmet.
Both types of stiffener are available in narrow widths, so the length can be cut from one piece without much wastage. Joins are best avoided as they have a tendency to create ridges and can reduce the stiffness of the pelmet.

☐ **Main pelmet fabric** Cut a piece of fabric 2.5cm larger than the pelmet template all round.
Plain fabrics can sometimes be cut along the length to avoid joins. If the fabric has a one-way design or a definite nap, however, you may need to join widths to make up a strip that is long enough for the pelmet. Join extra fabric to either side of a central fabric width using flat seams, and press seams open.

☐ **Lining** If using buckram or double-sided self-adhesive stiffener, cut a piece of lining material 1cm larger than the pelmet template all round.
☐ **Interlining** For a buckram pelmet, you also need a piece of bump or iron-on interfacing in the same shape and size as the template. If necessary, butt edges together and use herringbone stitch to join widths and make up pelmet length.

MAKING A PELMET WITH BUCKRAM

Buckram is quite stiff to handle, so make sure you use a strong, sharp needle when stitching by hand. You may also want to use a thimble.

1 Attach interlining ▷
Place interlining centrally on wrong side of pelmet fabric. Pin. Press iron-on interfacing into place. If using bump, lock stitch interlining to fabric.

Lock stitch Fold back the interlining 30cm from right hand edge, and lock stitch it to the pelmet fabric. Working from top to bottom edge of interlining, pick up a single thread from each layer of fabric. Place stitches about 10cm apart, and keep the thread fairly slack so that it doesn't pull the fabric. Fold interlining back over fabric, and work further lines of lock stitch 30cm apart along the length of the pelmet.

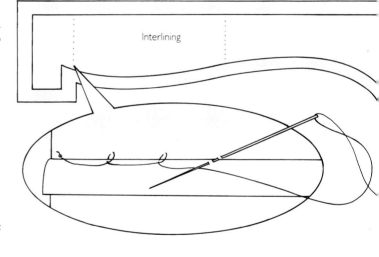

2 Attach buckram ▷
Place buckram centrally on top of interlining: pin, then tack through all the layers of fabric. Clip into the fabric seam allowance around curves and at corners, and trim away excess where necessary so that you can turn the border of fabric over the buckram.
If using iron-on buckram, dampen the edges and iron the fabric turnings in place. With ordinary buckram, pin and slipstitch the turned fabric to the buckram.

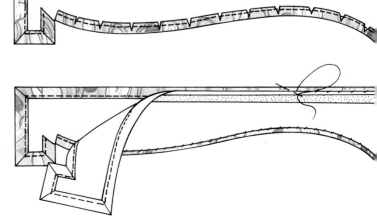

3 Sew lining to main fabric ▷
Turn in a 1.5cm seam allowance on lining fabric to make it 5mm smaller all round than the pelmet, clipping and trimming as necessary; tack and press. If you intend to hang the pelmet with Velcro (opposite), stitch the soft half of a strip of Velcro along top edge of right side of lining at this stage.
Then place lining, right side up, on top of buckram. Pin, tack and slipstitch all round, catching lining to the seam allowance of the main pelmet fabric.

MAKING A PELMET WITH DOUBLE-SIDED SELF-ADHESIVE STIFFENER

First cut out the stiffener, then cut fabric and lining – previous page.

BRIGHT IDEA

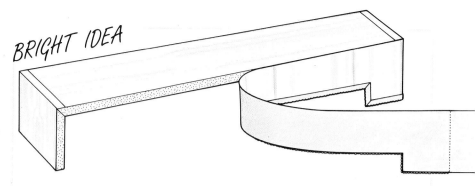

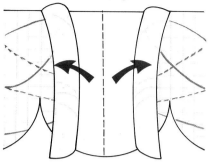

1 Remove backing paper △
Ease backing paper from centre of stiffener, cut it across the width and peel back a little on each side. Place wrong side of pelmet fabric centrally on top of exposed adhesive, and press down. Continue peeling away paper while smoothing down fabric, working from the centre outwards.

Clip into fabric seam allowance around curves and into corners, and fold to wrong side of pelmet. Peel backing off other side of stiffener and press down fabric turnings to stick.

2 Prepare lining material ▽
If hanging pelmet with Velcro, sew the soft half of Velcro to right side of lining 2.5cm from top edge. Press a 1.5cm turning to wrong side all round.

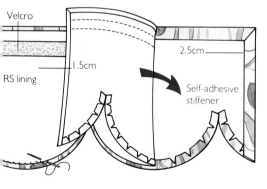

3 Stitch lining to pelmet
With wrong side of lining to wrong side of pelmet, smooth the lining down on to the adhesive surface, working from the centre outwards. Then slipstitch it to the main fabric all round.

For a neat finish, you can glue or slipstitch a decorative braid trim to the top and/or bottom of the pelmet, folding the braid into neat mitres at corners. Then hang the pelmet.

Smart stripes ▷
A simple classic pelmet shape complements a striped fabric. Here, the row of green braid along the bottom edge of the pelmet gives the shape definition without making it look heavy.

USE SINGLE-SIDED STIFFENER

The simplest and quickest way to make a pelmet is to use single-sided self-adhesive stiffener as it can be put together without any sewing, and does not require lining.

This type of pelmet is also very easy to hang, as you need attach only the coarser hooked side of a strip of Velcro to the pelmet board. The velour backing on single-sided stiffener clings to this and acts as the other half.

To make the pelmet Start by cutting the fabric 2cm larger all round than the pelmet. Cut the stiffener to shape: the backing is marked with a grid to make it easy to mark out a pattern. Then simply peel the printed backing paper off the strip of stiffener, and place the wrong side of the pelmet fabric on top – see Step 1, Making a pelmet with double-sided stiffener.

Press fabric down and smooth into place. Then use sharp scissors to trim the fabric edges flush to the pelmet shape. For a neat finish, stick a decorative braid or fringe over the cut edges of the pelmet with fabric adhesive.

MAKING CURTAIN VALANCES

Elegant and formal, or frilly and charming, a curtain valance adds a decorative feature to your window.

Curtain valances are often confused with pelmets, but a pelmet is a rigid fitting, either in wood or stiffened fabric, whereas a valance is a strip of fabric, gathered by hand or with heading tape. Like pelmets, valances are used to disguise the tops of curtains and the curtain track, or to enhance the proportions of a window, as well as for their decorative effect.

The valances discussed in this chapter can be hung above a curtain on tracks, wooden curtain poles, rods or a simple shelf-style fitting.

The style depends on the fabric the curtains are made from and the way the room is furnished. A simple gathered valance made from a printed cotton gives a country look, while a valance of regular or grouped pleats provides a more formal touch for heavier fabrics.

Proportion The depth of the valance depends on the proportions of the window as well as personal taste. For example, a deep valance tends to lower a tall, narrow window, and helps to obscure an unsightly view, while a shorter valance allows light in through a small or shaded window.

There are no hard and fast rules on the depth of valance, but bear in mind that, unless it is on a pole, it must cover the fitting or track on which it is hanging and the heading of the curtains. Start with the valance being one sixth of the curtain drop; this gives a point from which to work.

The right lines
This window has been fitted with a gathered, pencil pleated valance. It gives the window a smart finish, hiding the roller blind fitting as well as the curtain heading and track.

VALANCE FITTINGS

Rod or wire fitting (top left) If the valance is to hang within a recess, it can be made with a cased heading and threaded on to a rod or curtain wire that is drawn very taut.

Wooden curtain pole fitting (top right) A valance can be hung from rings on a decorative wooden curtain pole. The pole should be at least 12cm longer than the curtain track and project far enough to clear the curtains.

Shelf fittings An alternative is to fix a shelf supported by angle irons or wooden brackets above the curtain track. It should be 12cm longer than the curtain track (unless in a recess) and protrude from the wall by 4cm more than the track. The valance can be hung with curtain hooks fitted to screw eyes round the edge of the valance shelf (centre left), or it can be tacked to the side and front edges, and the tacks covered with braid, glued in place to hide the tack heads (centre right).

Valance track fittings (below right) Some manufacturers produce special valance tracks which are fitted to the curtain track with extended brackets to clear the curtains. The valance is then fitted to the track like a curtain, using curtain tape and hooks. It is not practical to fix valance track above decorative curtain poles.

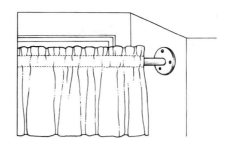

Rod fitting

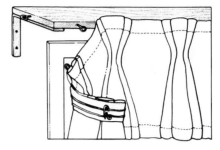

Shelf fitting with hooks

MEASURING UP

Cut a paper template to represent the valance, one sixth of the length of the curtain drop, pinning it in place over the top of the curtains. Then trim or lengthen the pattern to give the effect you want. Add a 2cm hem allowance. The top seam allowance depends on the heading, as does the width of fabric required.

Wooden pole fitting

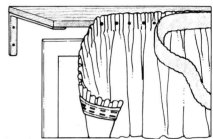

Shelf fitting with tacks

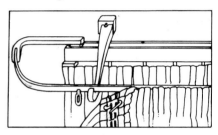

Valance track fitting

A CASED HEADING

This is the easiest valance to make and hang as the supporting rod, tube or wire is simply threaded through the cased heading.

How much fabric? To calculate the length of fabric required, decide on the depth of the pelmet as described earlier, adding a 6cm top seam allowance to make a casing for a rod up to 2cm in diameter.

To get the correct width of fabric allow for one and a half to two times the length of the rod, tube or wire.

1 *Cut out the fabric*
Cut out strips of fabric to the depth of the finished valance plus hem and heading allowances. Join strips to make one long valance, one-and-a-half to two times the length of the paper pattern. Use flat seams, neatening raw edges.

2 *Hem side and lower edges*
Turn a double hem (5mm, and then another 1cm) to the wrong side down each side edge of the valance, and machine stitch.

Turn a double 1cm hem (1cm, and then another 1cm) along the lower edge of the valance and stitch. Alternatively, you can trim off the lower seam allowance and bind the cut edge with a contrasting binding.

3 *Make a casing* ▽
Along the top edge, turn under the raw edge by 1cm and tack. Turn under a further 5cm seam allowance to the wrong side of the fabric, then stitch 5mm from the first fold. Then make another row of stitching 4cm above this one to form a casing for the rod.

Press well and add trimmings before threading the valance on to the rod.

CHECK YOUR NEEDS
☐ Fabric
☐ Lining (optional)
☐ Iron-on interfacing (optional)
☐ Curtain heading tape (optional)
☐ Hooks or tacks (optional)
☐ Paper for pattern (optional)
plus:
☐ Steel tape
☐ Tape measure
☐ Tailor's chalk
☐ Scissors
☐ Pins
☐ Needles
☐ Sewing thread
☐ Sewing machine
☐ Iron
☐ Ironing board

A simple gathered heading
This method can be adapted for a simple gathered heading attached around a shelf fitting. Instead of adding a second row of stitching along the top edge, make two rows of gathering stitches and pull up to fit the shelf.

Nail in place round edge of shelf and cover the nail heads with braid, or bias binding. Glue in place with fabric adhesive, turning under ends to neaten.

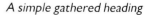
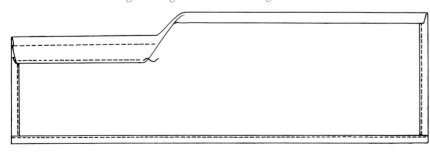

VALANCES WITH HEADING TAPE

This style of valance is made up in the same way as a short curtain – with either a gathered, pencil-pleated or triple-pleated heading, depending on the curtain heading tape you use.

It can be made like an unlined curtain or it can be given more body with iron-on interfacing, in which case it should be lined for a neat finish.

How much fabric? The depth of fabric required is as described before plus a top seam allowance of 4cm.

The width of fabric depends on the manufacturer's recommendation for the type of heading tape used. Standard heading tape requires at least one-and-a-half times the length of the track; others require more.

AN UNLINED VALANCE

This type of valance is straightforward to make, and gives an easy, informal look to a window. Use a standard heading tape to emphasize the effect.

1 Cut fabric
Cut out the fabric to the required measurements, and join widths if necessary with 1.5cm flat seams. Cut heading tape to right length

2 Attach heading tape
Neaten the side and lower edges of the valance as for a cased heading (see Step 2). At the top of the valance, turn 4cm to the wrong side and press. Pin heading tape in place on wrong side of valance to cover the raw hem edge.

Turn in the raw ends of the tape – but not the pulling up cords – and tack, then stitch in place.

3 Hang the valance ▽
Pull up the cords until the valance is the right width and tie the ends to secure. Even out the gathers, insert curtain hooks and hang the valance as if it were a curtain.

For a shelf fitment, line up the curtain tape with the edges of the shelf and attach with upholstery tacks. Cover tack heads with braid.

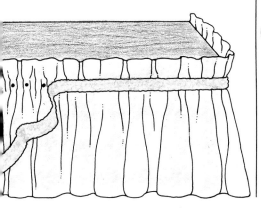

AN INTERFACED VALANCE

An iron-on interfacing can be used to give the valance more body and a much crisper look. The finish is more suited to formal styles – pencil or pinch pleated headings. There are several weights of interfacing – so select the weight that, together with your fabric, gives the desired thickness.

A lining gives your curtain valance a much tidier looking finish when viewed from outside, and also helps to protect it from sunlight. Choose lining to match curtain lining.

1 Cut out the fabric
Cut out the main valance fabric to the required length and width plus seam allowances in exactly the same way as for an unlined valance. Then cut the lining and interlining to the exact finished measurements, this time without seam allowances. If necessary, join the fabric widths and lining widths with 1.5cm flat seams.

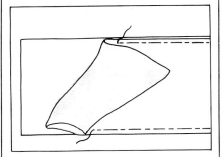

2 Attach interfacing and lining △
Position the interfacing on the wrong side of the valance fabric so that it lies within the seam allowances. Dry iron in place, following the manufacturer's instructions for heat setting. Tack the lining in place, matching the edges of the lining to the edges of the interfacing.

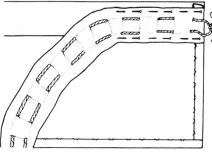

3 Attach heading tape △
Turn under double hems along the side and lower edges of the valance, as for the cased valance (see Step 2), so the hems overlap the lining. Pin and slipstitch down to the lining. Finally turn down the same allowance along the top edge and pin, tack and stitch the heading tape in place.

A VALANCE WITH A HAND-PLEATED HEADING

A hand-pleated valance should be interfaced and lined, as with the interfaced valance with heading tape.

How much fabric? To get the length of fabric, measure the depth of the valance and add 2cm for the lower seam allowance plus 4cm for the top seam.

For the width measure the length of the rod or pole. Then use a strip of paper to work out the size and type of pleat that will suit your valance and fit evenly into its length. Three times the finished width, plus seam allowances is needed for continuous pleats.

1 Cut fabric
Cut fabric to required measurements. Then cut lining and interfacing to exact finished measurements (without seam allowances). Make up the valance in the same way as the lined version with heading tape but, after folding over top, do not add heading tape.

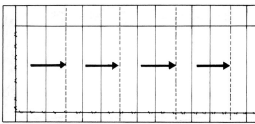

2 Mark out the pleats △
Following the pleat size from your experimental paper strip, mark out the valance into even divisions using tailor's chalk on wrong side of fabric.

Fold and press the pleats, one by one, and pin and tack in position.

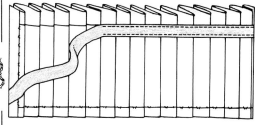

3 Attach tape △
Pin a length of plain tape, about 2.5cm wide, over the raw hem edge at the top on the wrong side of the valance, and stitch in place. You can hand sew the tape if you don't want the stitching lines to show on the right side, but be sure to stitch through all but the front layer of fabric in order to secure the pleats. If necessary neatly catchstitch the top edges of the pleats together on the right side to ensure a crisp finish.

Sew rings or hooks to the tape to attach the valance to its support.

FINISHES FOR STRAIGHT VALANCES

However the valance is made, and whatever method of fixing you choose, you can add decorative trims to add extra interest at the top of the window, and to create a definite division between the valance and the curtains.

Adding a frill A frill can be added for a feminine, country finish. Once the valance has been made up, cut a strip one-and-a-half times the length of the flat valance, and about 7cm deep. Join lengths with flat seams, neatening seam allowances. Turn under a 1cm double hem along lower and side edges. Run two lines of gathering stitches along frill, about 1cm from top. Draw up gathers to fit, then, right sides facing, pin, tack and stitch 4cm from lower edge of valance, stitching along gathering, distributing fullness evenly.

Bound edges Once you have made up your valance, you can bind it with bias binding or a broader strip of bias or straight cut contrasting fabric.

Fringes and tassels You can also buy ready-made decorative fringes which can be used down the length of curtains as well as along the lower edge of the valance. For a tailored effect, stitch the fringe to the valance so that the lower edge of the fringing is level with the lower edge of the valance.

▽ *Triple pleats*

This valance has been triple pleated, using a heading tape. The valance is interfaced, and the hem left unpressed to soften the effect.

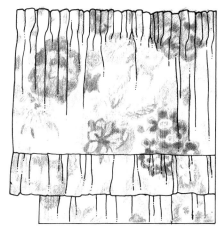

△ *Valance with frill*

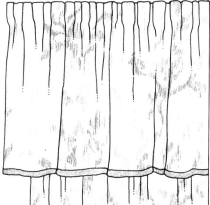

△ *Valance with bias binding*

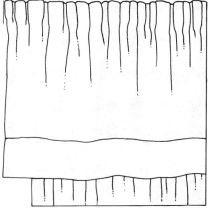

△ *Valance with contrasting fabric*

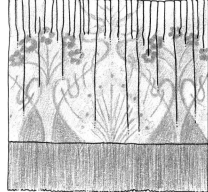

△ *Valance with fringed edging*

SOFTER SHAPES FOR VALANCES

For luxurious effects, go to town with clever shapes and flounces to frame your windows.

In formally-furnished or cottage-style rooms, you can set the style with an extravagant curved valance to top off your windows. The effects and details are almost limitless: tight gathers, formal pleats, piping, frills, contrast lining, or neat boxed headings.

CHOOSE YOUR FABRICS

In most cases the valances look best if they match the curtains: choose cotton sateen and glazed cottons, plain repps and slub weaves or damasks. Velvet pile fabrics are not so suitable for these elaborate effects. A fabric with a sheen to it will show off the gathers better, and look more luxurious. If you are adding frills and piping, these often look best in a contrasting colour – so look out for suitable fabrics of a similar weight for trims. Bear in mind that, with

several layers of fabric to stitch in some of the seams, you should avoid very thick fabrics which will give unmanageable bulk.

Most of the effects described here look best lined. Curtain lining fabric comes in a wide range of colours, with the darker shades giving a richer look. Paler ones are more suitable if you are trying to achieve a fresh, cottage style. However, you are not restricted to using lining fabric: since the 'wrong' side is often on view almost as much as the 'right' side, if your budget allows, line valances with the same fabric that you choose for trims such as frills and piping.

Co-ordinating the effect To enhance the effect, choose fabrics to co-ordinate with other furnishings in the room: for example, in the bedroom shown here, a striped fabric has been used to line and

trim a flowery valance. The curtains are in the same floral fabric, with the tiebacks in the striped fabric, matching the blind. Elsewhere in the room, it would be a good idea to have furnishings in the same, matching fabrics. For example, combine pink and white candy-striped bedlinen, with a floral quilted bedspread, or a bedroom chair upholstered in stripes, with floral, frilled cushions, piped with the pink striped fabric.

MEASURING UP

As with pelmets and gathered valances, the finished length of the valance is the length round the pelmet shelf, or across the front of the alcove of a recessed window. Once you have decided where the valance is to hang, put up the necessary fixings. Often, the simplest solution is a pelmet shelf, fitted on angle irons above the window, with the valance fitted to screw eyes round the shelf and the curtains fitted to tracks under the shelf.

As with plain valances, there are no rules as to the depth of the valance, or the shape. Normally, you don't want a valance to hang more than a sixth of the way down the window. However, it could be curved to hang a third or half-way down at the sides of the window.

To finalize the shape of the valance, it is necessary to sketch out some designs, copying them from pictures if you see exactly what you want. Then, the easiest way to transfer the sketch to the fabric for cutting out is to make a pattern for a pelmet, and 'spread' it to give you the necessary allowance for gathering the heading. 'Spreading' involves measuring the pattern at even intervals, and marking the measurements on to a second pattern, spacing them farther apart.

Before you can finalize the amount of fabric, you must decide on the heading of the valance: an easy way to make a neat heading is to use pencil-pleated curtain heading tape. For a luxurious effect, make the valance three times the length round the pelmet shelf. An alternative finish, described in detail here, is to gather the valance and fit it to a box heading. One advantage of this finish is that you can use Velcro tape to hold up the valance – this saves on curtains hooks and screw eyes, and prevents the valance sagging.

All dressed up
An ordinary window becomes special with a frilled valance tumbling down to frame the window and dressing table. Note how the valance is lined with the same fabric used to make up the frill.

CHECK YOUR NEEDS

To make the pattern:
☐ Paper and pencil
☐ Wall lining paper
☐ Scissors (for paper)
☐ Tape measure
☐ Ruler

To cut out and make up valance:
☐ Fabric
☐ Fabric(s) for lining and trims
☐ Ruler and tape measure
☐ Dressmaker's chalk
☐ Scissors
☐ Sewing machine
☐ Pins and needles

☐ Iron and ironing board
☐ Interlining (optional)
☐ Piping cord (optional)

To hang the valance:
☐ Heading tape, curtain hooks and screw eyes OR
☐ Velcro and staple gun

DESIGNING A SHAPED VALANCE

To finalize the shape of the valance and check that the planned depth is suitable, it is best to make a paper pattern first.

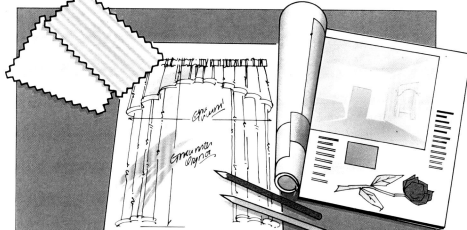

1 Sketch out a shape ▷
Sketch out your ideas for a shaped valance, copying and adapting from favourite pictures or from ideas you have seen in showrooms. Mark in accurate measurements of your window, and approximate measurements for the valance. Choose the fabrics you want, and get hold of small samples if possible to check colour and effect.

2 Draw out the pattern ▷
Using a piece of wall lining paper, sketch out the approximate shape and actual size you want the valance to be, making use of a flexible curve (a wire-reinforced rubber ruler). At this stage, do not include any allowance for gathers or frills. These are added later.

3 Cut out the pattern
Hold up your sketch in position at the top of the window. It will be easier to judge the finished effect if the pelmet shelf is in place and the curtains are already hung. If you think your sketch looks promising, fold the paper in half down the middle and cut through both thicknesses together to ensure the pattern is symmetrical.

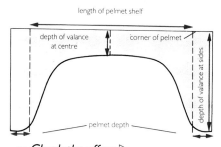

length of pelmet shelf

depth of valance at centre

corner of pelmet

depth of valance at sides

pelmet depth

4 Check the effect ▷
Use masking tape to hold the pattern up to check the effect again. If you are happy, use this pattern, otherwise trim it as necessary, or trace it out again adding depth and shaping where needed. If you are going to add frills, these hang down below the main fabric of the valance, so bear this in mind when finalizing your design.

CUTTING OUT THE FABRIC

1 Calculate the amount of fabric
From your pattern, work out the overall dimensions of the fabric needed for the valance. This will be three times the width of the valance pattern, plus 3cm for turnings, by the depth of the valance, plus 3cm for turnings. For a double thickness frill, 6cm wide, you will need a strip of fabric 15cm wide by six times the measurement of the long, shaped edge of the pattern.

2 Prepare the fabric
Using flat seams, join up sufficient widths of fabric and lining to make panels the overall size of the valance, plus a 1.5cm seam allowance all round.

3 Spread the pattern ▷
Cut another piece of lining paper one-and-a-half times the length of the first, plus 1.5cm seam allowance at one end. Fold the first pattern in half down the centre. Measure the depth of the pattern at each end, and at 5cm intervals across its width. Add 3cm allowance to these depths. Mark the depths on the second pattern. Position the mark for deepest measurement, 1.5cm from the end of the second pattern, and the centre mark at the other end. Space the intervening marks 15cm apart rather than the 5cm that they were on the first pattern. Now draw a gentle curve through the marks, to give you the cutting line.

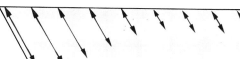

4 Cut out the fabric
Lay the second pattern on the folded fabric, with the short end of the pattern on the fold line. Pin in place, then tack the layers of fabric together and cut out. Repeat for the lining. Cut out sufficient 15cm-wide strips of fabric to make up the frill.

MAKING UP A FRILLED VALANCE

These instructions are for a deeply shaped valance, with one double-thickness frill set into the lower edge.

There is no reason why you shouldn't adapt the design, adding a second, deeper frill, or binding the edges of the valance. Bear in mind that with bound edges you do not need the 1.5cm seam allowance which has been included. With the fabric cut out, making up the valance is straightforward.

1 *Prepare the frill ▷*
Join up the strips of fabric for the frill, using flat seams; press open. Fold the frill in half along its length, right sides facing, and stitch across ends, 1.5cm from raw edges. Trim seam allowance, clip across corner to help the end of the frill to lie flat and turn right side out. Press to make a frill 7.5cm wide with a folded edge.

2 *Gather the frill*
Run two lines of gathering stitches along the long, unfinished edge of the frill, through both layers of fabric, within 1.5cm of the edge. Draw up frill to match curved edge of valance, leaving free 1.5cm at each end of the valance for seams.

3 *Make up the valance △*
Lay the valance fabric on a flat surface, right side up. Position the frill along the shaped edge, raw edges matching, ensuring the ends of the frill are clear of the seam allowance at the ends of the valance. Pin and tack in place, distributing fullness evenly. Lay the lining fabric on top of the valance fabric, right sides facing and raw edges matching, sandwiching the frill in place. Pin and tack in place all round, taking care not to catch side edges of frill in the seam.

4 *Stitch the seam*
Stitch all round the valance, leaving a 20cm opening in the top edge. Trim seam allowance, particularly along the frill. Clip seam allowance at corners. Turn right side out. Turn in and press seam allowance along opening.

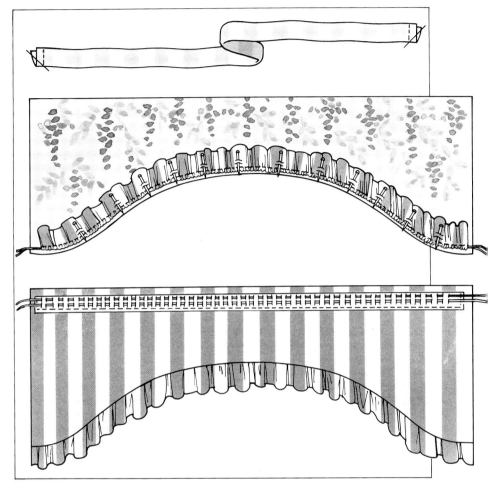

5 *Attach heading tape △*
Cut the heading tape so that it is about 4cm longer than the width of the valance. Turn under 2cm at each end. Pin in place, positioning the top of the tape 5mm from the top of the valance. Ease the cords out from the ends of the tape where it is turned under. Tack, then stitch, leaving ends of cord free.

6 *Draw up the cords*
Draw up the cords until the valance is drawn up to a third of its width, and matches the length of the pelmet shelf. Knot the cords, and carry the ends to one side, pinning or tacking them in place so they don't dangle below the valance.

BRIGHT IDEA

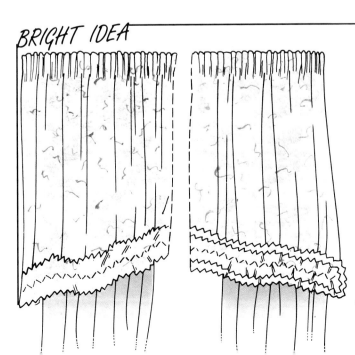

Quick frills Frills with pinked edges are a quick alternative to a double frill. Make up the valance as described above, without the frill sandwiched in the curved seam. Cut strips of fabric, 6cm wide, with pinking shears. Make a single line of gathering stitches along the centre of the frill, draw it up slightly (it need not be as much as twice the fullness of the valance) and pin it to the lower edge of the valance. Tack, then stitch in place with a zigzag stitch.

You can use the same technique to add a double frill, cutting an 8cm-wide strip in contrast fabric and a 6cm-wide strip in fabric to match the valance. Lay the narrower strip on top of the wider one, then gather and stitch them to the valance as though they were a single strip.

Alternatively, cut a 5cm wide frill. Pink one long edge, gather the other edge and set into the valance.

SHAPED VALANCE WITH BOXED HEADING

Rather than making a heading with curtain tape, and attaching the valance to screw eyes, you can gather the valance on to a boxed heading and attach it to the pelmet shelf with Velcro. The boxed section is interlined for a soft finish, and the lower edge bound with contrast fabric as an alternative to a frilled edge. Piping round the edge of the boxed heading makes a neat finish.

1 Prepare the pattern
Draw up a pelmet pattern, as for a shaped pelmet (see page 32). Cut 10cm off the top of the pattern.

2 Calculating fabric
For the gathered section of the valance, you need a panel of fabric three times the length of the pattern, plus 3cm seam allowance, by the depth of the pattern plus 1.5cm seam allowance along the top edge. You also need a strip of fabric for the boxed section, the same length as the paper pattern, plus 3cm seam allowance, by 13cm (for a 10cm deep box). You need enough piping cord and 3.5cm wide bias-cut piping to go all round the box. For binding the lower edge you need a 7cm wide bias-cut strip, the same length as the curved lower edge of the valance (see page 37 for details of cutting bias strips).

3 Cut out the fabric
Join up panels of fabric and lining to make a strip three times the length of your paper pattern, by its trimmed depth plus 1.5cm seam allowance along the top edge. Fold the pelmet pattern in half and 'spread' it to allow for gathers as described on page 32, adding 1.5cm seam allowance. Place the valance pattern on folded fabric and cut out as before. Cut out strips of fabric and lining for the box section, joining widths if necessary. Cut out bias-cut piping to fit all round the boxed section, and binding strips to fit along the lower edge of the valance. Join up strips as necessary, and prepare piping.

4 Make up gathered section
Lay valance fabric on top of lining, right sides together and raw edges matching. Stitch together down side edges. Turn right side out and press. Tack fabric to lining along lower edge, then bind it, taking 1.5cm seams and slipstitching the binding in place on the back of the valance. Neaten ends of binding by slipstitching in place. Run two lines of gathering stitches along top edge.

5 Interline the box section
Cut a piece of interlining the same size as the finished box section. If you need to join strips of interlining fabric, make as flat a seam as possible by overlapping the selvedges by about 7mm; then pin, tack and zig zag stitch through both layers. Lay the interlining on the wrong side of the panel of fabric for the box section, leaving a 1.5cm seam allowance all round. Hold in place with herringbone stitch.

6 Add the piping
Lay out the fabric, right side up, and position piping round panel, raw edges matching. Clip into seam allowance of piping at corners. Pin, tack and stitch in place. Lay the lining on top of the piped panel, right sides facing and raw edges matching. Pin, tack and stitch lining to fabric, enclosing piping, round side and upper edges. Trim seam allowances, clip corners and turn right side out. Press under seam allowances along lower edge.

7 Set in the gathered valance
Draw up gathering stitches so that the top edge of the gathered section matches the lower edge of the boxed section. With right sides of fabric facing and raw edges matching, pin the gathered section to the box section, sandwiching the piping. Distribute gathers evenly, then tack and stitch in place. Stitch folded edge of lining to seamline by hand.

8 Add the Velcro
Pin the furry half of the Velcro to the back of the boxed section, positioning the top edge of it level with the top of the lining. Stitch the Velcro in place by hand, just catching the front of the fabric so that the valance cannot roll down and show the lining, or sag away from the pelmet shelf when fixed in place. Staple the hooked half of the Velcro round the edge of the pelmet shelf, using a staple gun.

◁ **All boxed up**
This gently-shaped valance has a boxed heading, which is piped all round for a neat finish. Interlining the boxed section adds a touch of luxury, and broad binding along the lower, curved edge adds to the crisp, tailored look of the valance.

TAILORED SHAPED CURTAIN TIEBACKS

Tiebacks are an easy way to dress up curtains. They are also pretty and practical.

Curtain tiebacks can be made up in a variety of shapes and styles, with different trims to suit your personal taste. They are easy and inexpensive to make yourself and can give a new lease of life to dull or old curtains.

If you are making tiebacks to add to existing curtains, don't worry if you have not got any of the original fabric. In fact, even if you have a remnant of fabric which matches, the chances are that the curtains will have faded, so the remnant will no longer match. You only need a remnant of fabric to achieve some dramatic effects – if you cannot match it to the curtains exactly, create added interest with contrasting fabric.

You can make perfectly plain straight tiebacks, but they work more effectively and look better if you shape them to give a more tailored finish. For a distinctive finish, pipe or bind the edges or add a frill all along the lower edge of the tieback.

CHOOSING FABRICS
Most light- or medium-weight, closely woven furnishing fabrics are suitable. Don't try to use heavy brocades or velvet as they are too bulky and won't make up successfully. Both sides of the tieback can be of furnishing fabric, or you can use lining fabric for the backing if you haven't got enough, or if the fabric is too bulky or rather expensive.

MEASURING UP
To calculate where to place the tieback and how long and how wide it should be, loop a tape measure around the curtain about two-thirds of the way down from the top and create the folds or the draped effect you want to achieve. Note the measurement on the tape measure as this will be the length of the finished tieback.

While the tape measure is still in place, make a small pencil mark on the wall or window surround to indicate the position for the fixing hook.

For sill-length curtains, the depth of the tieback should be no more than 10cm, but for longer curtains it may be enlarged proportionally. Instructions given here are for 10cm deep tiebacks. Seams throughout are 1.5cm unless otherwise stated.

Tidy lines
A perfect solution for a graceful, arched window: the curtains are fitted to the top of the window frame, and rather than opening on a track they are held open by the tiebacks. In this case, the chair rail has been used as a fixing point for the tiebacks, almost exactly a third of the way up the window. The bound edges emphasize the shape of the tiebacks.

MAKING A STRAIGHT-EDGED TIEBACK

1 *Cut out a pattern*
Start by drawing a rectangle on a sheet of paper: the length should be the same as the length you measured with the tape measure, and the depth should be 10cm. Cut out.

2 *Cut out the fabrics*
For each tieback, pin the pattern to a double thickness of fabric and cut out, (or cut out once in fabric and once in lining), allowing an extra 1.5cm all round for seams.
Pin the pattern to a single thickness of interfacing and cut out without any seam allowance.

CHECK YOUR NEEDS
- ☐ Fabric
- ☐ Lining (optional)
- ☐ Interfacing – use pelmet buckram or firm Vilene interfacing for straight and shaped tiebacks or iron-on interfacing for bows
- ☐ Four small curtain rings
- ☐ Two hooks for fixing to wall
- ☐ Sewing thread
- ☐ Needle
- ☐ Paper for patterns
- ☐ Iron and ironing board
- ☐ Scissors
- ☐ Tape measure
- ☐ Pins

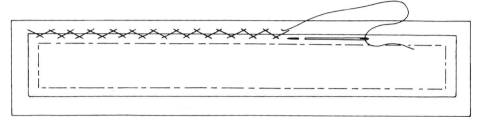

3 *Attach the interfacing* △
Lay the interfacing centrally on the wrong side of one piece of fabric. Tack in place. Herringbone stitch all round the edges of the interfacing to catch to fabric. Work the herringbone stitch

from left to right, first taking a small stitch horizontally in the tieback fabric and then diagonally lower down on the interfacing. The stitches should not show on the right side of the tieback fabric.

MAKING SHAPED TIEBACKS

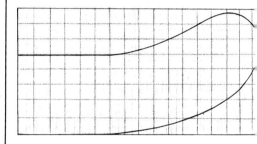

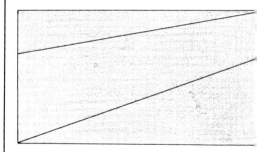

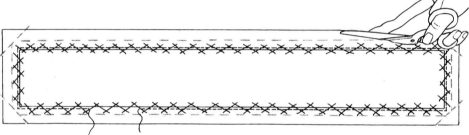

4 *Make up the tieback* △
Place the two tieback pieces right sides facing and tack together all round, leaving a 10cm gap for turning through to the right side. Machine with the interfacing uppermost, being careful to sew close to, but not over, the edge of

the interfacing.
Trim the seams and clip diagonally across the corners. Remove tacking. Turn through to right side and slipstitch the open edges together to close. Press.
Make up a second tieback to match in the same way.

1 *Draw up the design* △
Measure the length of the tieback as before. Cut a piece of graph paper printed with 1cm squares the length of the tieback by at least 15cm deep and fold in half widthways. Either follow one of the charts here for a simply-shaped tieback, or draw out your own design. Cut out the pattern, open flat and hold in place to check that the shape is effective.

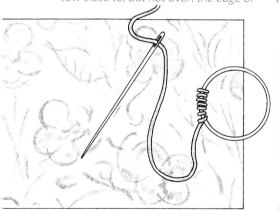

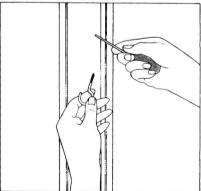

5 *Attach the rings* △
Sew a curtain ring to the middle of each short edge. Working on the wrong side of the fabric, overcast the ring just inside the edge so that enough of the ring protrudes to fit neatly over the hook which will be fixed to the wall.

6 *Fix hooks to hold tiebacks* △
Fix a hook to hold the tiebacks in place where the mark is. If the window surround is wood, you can simply use a cup hook, making a small pilot hole with a bradawl first.
If there is a plaster finish at the point where the tieback is to be fixed, you will have to drill and fit a wallplug.

2 *Cut out the fabrics*
Cut out twice in fabric (or once in fabric and once in lining) with a seam allowance and once in interfacing without seam allowance for each tieback.

3 *Make up the tiebacks*
Make up the tiebacks and attach rings and hooks as for straight-edged tiebacks, following the instructions in step 6.

TRIMS FOR TIEBACKS

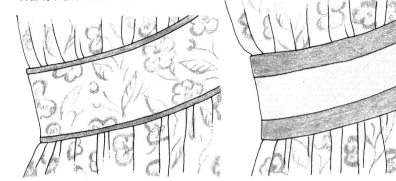

Piped edges Piping in the seam line emphasizes shape and can at the same time provide a contrast colour. Either cover the piping cord with bias strips cut from the same fabric as the tieback or use purchased bias binding, 2.5cm wide. Cover the cord and apply to the right side of one piece of the tieback, raw edges together. Continue making up the tieback as before, sandwiching the piping between the two layers of fabric. Use a zipper foot to sew the seam, stitching as close to the piping as possible. (For more information about working the piping, see Making Cushions, page 70.)

Bound edges Binding all round the edges gives the chance to introduce a contrast colour, or to pick up a plain colour from a patterned fabric. Again, you can use bias strips cut from the fabric or purchased bias binding. Cut out the fabric and interfacing to shape you require, without any seam allowance.

With wrong sides facing, sandwich the interfacing between the two pieces of fabric, and tack together around the edges. Round off any corners slightly to make it easier to apply the binding. Attach bias strips or bias binding, slipstitching in place on the wrong side (see below).

Frilled edges Measure along the bottom edge of the tieback and cut a 7.5cm wide strip of fabric twice this measurement. Turn under double hem along one long edge and two short edges of the frill. Sew two lines of gathering threads along the remaining raw edge. Place the frill on one tieback piece, right sides facing and with raw edge of frill matching lower raw edge of tieback. Pin each end of the frill 1.5cm in from the side edges of the tieback, and pull up the gathering threads until the frill fits along the edge of the tieback. Tack in place. Continue to make up the tieback as for the straight version.

USING BIAS BINDING

Using bias strips means that you can ease the binding round gently curved shapes, such as tailored tiebacks, because fabric that is cut diagonally will stretch and give slightly.

Most commercially-available bias binding is made from a 3.5cm strip of fabric, folded in half down its length, with 5mm turnings pressed under along each long raw edge.

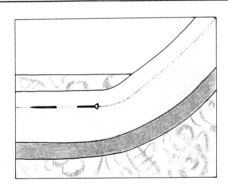

1 *Stitch to right side △*
Open out the bias strip, and with right sides facing, pin, tack and stitch along the fold line of the binding.

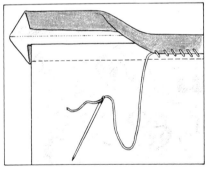

2 *Slipstitch in place △*
Turn binding over the edge of the fabric. Slipstitch the folded edge to wrong side, just inside row of stitches.

CUTTING YOUR OWN BIAS STRIPS

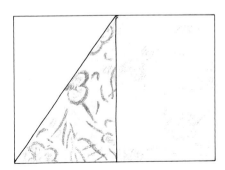

1 *Mark the diagonal △*
Choose fabric to match or contrast with the tieback or item you are sewing.
Find the bias or cross of the fabric by laying the fabric flat, and folding one corner at a 45° angle. Press.

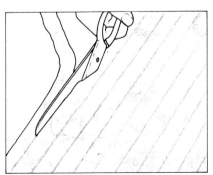

2 *Cut the strips △*
Mark a series of lines parallel to this fold line, at least 3.5cm apart, depending on the finished effect you want. Cut along marked lines.

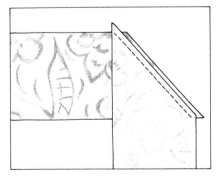

3 *Joining strips △*
If you need to join bias strips, place the two strips to be joined at right angles to each other, with right sides facing. Sew with a narrow (5mm) flat seam. Press seam open.

MAKING A SCALLOPED TIEBACK

1 Draw up the basic shape
Draw up a pattern for the basic shape of tieback you require, following the instructions for shaped tiebacks on the previous page. Use a folded sheet of graph paper at least 20cm wide marked with 1cm squares.

2 Mark in the scallops ▽
Using a suitable size curve – an egg cup or the rim of a small wine glass – draw a series of even-sized scallop shapes along the lower edge of the paper pattern. Start with a full scallop at the fold and, when you reach the end,

adjust to finish with either a half or a complete scallop, or draw a shallower scallop to fill the space if you prefer. Adjust the scallops until you are happy with the effect. You can make progressively shallower scallops if you prefer a tapered look.

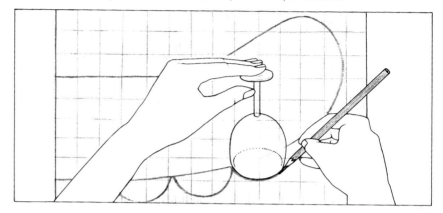

3 Cut out the pattern and fabric
Cut out the paper pattern and open out flat. For each tieback, cut out twice in fabric or once in fabric and once in lining with an additional 1.5cm all round for the seam allowance. Cut out in interfacing.

4 Make up the tiebacks
Continue to make up the tiebacks as before, sewing carefully around the scallop shapes. Snip into seam allowance on curves and turn to right side.

QUICK SCALLOPED TIEBACKS

1 Draw the template
Draw the template up on graph paper using an egg cup or wine glass to make the scalloped shapes as before.

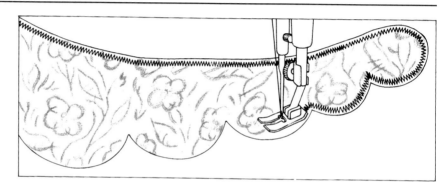

2 Cut out the fabric
Cut out twice in fabric, allowing a 1cm seam allowance all round, and once in interfacing.

3 Attach the interfacing
Attach the interfacing to the wrong side of one piece of fabric as before, then, with wrong sides facing, pin, tack and stitch the fabric pieces together, sandwiching the interfacing, stitching close to the edge of the interfacing.

4 Finish the edges △
Set your machine to a closed-up zigzag stitch or satin stitch. Zigzag stitch round the edge of the tieback following the seam line. As an alternative, you can zigzag the edges of the scallops with a contrasting coloured sewing thread.

5 Trim the edges
Use a small pair of sewing scissors to trim the seam allowance close to the stitching, making sure you do not cut any of the stitches. Repeat for the second tieback and add rings.

BRIGHT IDEA

RIBBON DEVELOPMENT ◁
If you haven't the time to make your own tiebacks, improvise by using a broad, good quality satin or velvet ribbon. Trim the edges diagonally or into a deep V shape to prevent fraying, and add a ring at the centre of the ribbon to hang it on a hook.

LACY DAYS ▷
Another trick is to use a length of broderie anglaise. It will look especially pretty on fresh cotton print curtains, and will add a touch of femininity to otherwise ordinary curtains. Use pre-gathered broderie anglaise to save extra sewing. To introduce some colour, use double-edged, ungathered broderie anglaise with eyelets and thread the eyelets with a thin piece of ribbon to match the curtains.

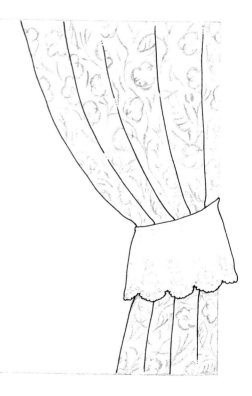

DRAPED SWAGS AND TAILS

For a dramatic effect at your windows dress them up with swags and tails — fabric draped around the top and sides.

Swags and tails have had their place in grand country houses for centuries, but there is no reason why you should not adapt the style to dress up windows on a smaller scale. However, they are extravagant in their use of fabric, and can be difficult to drape effectively, so it is not a project for someone who is inexperienced at home sewing.

Choosing fabrics The fabrics you use will depend on the finished effect you are aiming for: traditional curtain fabrics create a formal atmosphere, but you could use finer fabrics or even muslin or sheer curtain fabric for a fantasy effect. Avoid using heavy fabrics such as linen unions or velvets.

Formal swags and tails should be lined to add to the luxurious effect and help them to hang properly. Also, bear in mind that the back of the swags are visible where they fold back on themselves, so a contrast lining and bound edge can produce an effective finish.

Suitable windows This type of finish is best suited to larger windows, since not only is it a particularly grand style, it also cuts down on the amount of light coming through the window. As well as the swags across the top of the window and tails down the side, you will probably want some other form of screening at the window: traditionally the choice is lined curtains with a pencil-pleated heading (see Simple Unlined Curtains and Curtains with Sewn-in Linings, pages 7-14) and tiebacks to hold the curtains in place (see pages 35-38). For a more up-to-the-minute look, you could install blinds or sheer curtains, or leave the windows uncurtained if you have a pleasant outlook and are not overlooked.

Proportions To ensure you don't end up with skimpy tails, they should fall about two-thirds of the way down the window. However, the swag should not drape more than a sixth of the way down the window, to avoid cutting out daylight. But there are no hard and fast rules: you will have to make a pattern from a spare piece of fabric and be prepared to tack it up more than once until you are satisfied with the effect.

FITTING AND MEASURING

The swags and tails are fitted to a pelmet shelf above the window — if you don't have one already, then the first thing to do is to fit one – see Traditional Fabric Pelmets. The swags and tails are held to the top of the pelmet shelf with Velcro – or they may be stapled in place if you are not going to want to take them down regularly to clean them.

Start by looking at plenty of pictures to get an idea of the different styles and shapes you can create: the line drawings overleaf give you a selection of ideas.

Once you have decided on the effect you want, measure up carefully: each swag and each tail is made up as a separate piece, but the aim is to create an illusion that the whole thing is made from one piece of fabric.

Sunny and elegant
Triple swags and softly-pleated tails in crisp cream cotton help to create a sunny feeling in this drawing room. Note that the tails have dark blue linings for extra definition.

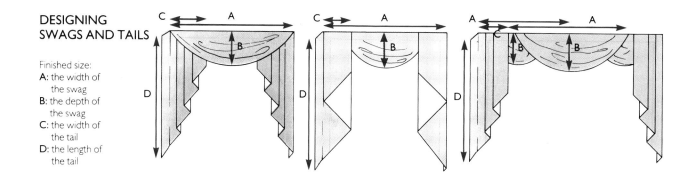

DESIGNING SWAGS AND TAILS

Finished size:
A: the width of the swag
B: the depth of the swag
C: the width of the tail
D: the length of the tail

CHECK YOUR NEEDS

☐ Pencil and paper
☐ Tape measure
☐ Lengths of lining, muslin or old sheets for making pattern
☐ Staple gun
☐ Fabric for swags and tails
☐ Fabric for lining/binding
☐ Velcro fastening
☐ Pins and needles
☐ Sewing machine
☐ Sewing thread
☐ Dressmaker's chalk

CALCULATING FABRIC AMOUNTS

Measure up and draw a plan of your window, then sketch in the effect you want before calculating how much fabric you need.

1 *Finished size of the swags*
First decide on the total length you want the swags to cover, ensuring the ends will be tucked well under the tails, or hidden over the top of the pelmet shelf. At the same time, decide how far down the window you want the swags to hang. The diagrams above give some idea of the different shapes to go for.

2 *Amount of fabric for the swags*
Calculate approximately how much fabric you will need, so you can make a pattern. The length of fabric for the swags is equal to the finished length of the swags, plus 3cm seam allowance and 5–10cm to allow the fabric to drape at the centre of the window. The width of fabric needed is 1½ times the finished depth of the swag, plus 3cm seam allowance and a 5cm allowance to go over the top of the pelmet shelf. You will need the same amount of fabric for lining. The ends will eventually be cut at an angle (see steps 5 and 6).

3 *Finished size of the tails*
Decide on the style and finished size of the tails: how far you want them to hang down the window, how many pleats you want, and what width you want them to be. In the example here, there are four folds, creating two pleats,

but you can make up your own variations. The secret of getting well-balanced folds is to cut the lower edge of the fabric on the bias. (This can be a bit wasteful, so try to find a use for the triangle you have to cut off.)

The pelmet shelf usually protrudes

from the wall, and the tails should wrap round the ends of the shelf (the return) to butt up against the wall. This gives a neat finish when you see the window from one side. Measure the depth of the pelmet shelf, so you can allow for the return.

4 *Amount of fabric for the tails*
For each tail you will need a length of fabric equal to the finished length of the tail, plus an allowance equal to the depth of the pelmet shelf at the top to allow for fixing, and a 3cm allowance for

seams. The width is three times the width of the pleated section of the tail, plus the width of any unpleated section. Add an allowance for the return down the outer edge of the swag if needed and a 3cm seam allowance.

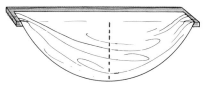

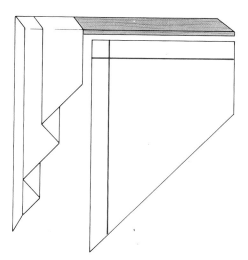

5 *Make pattern for the swag △*
To guarantee that your swags and tails will drape well, use some lining fabric, muslin, or even an old sheet to make a pattern. This is essential if you want to make a series of swags across the top of the window. Use the calculations in steps 1 and 2 to work out the approximate dimensions and cut a piece of fabric for the pattern, omitting the seam allowances along the top and bottom edges, but allowing an extra 5–10cm at each end. Mark the centre of

the swag on the piece of fabric for the pattern. Drape the fabric across the top of the window where the swag is to go, and gather or pleat the ends in place. You will find that you need to make the lines of gathering stitching at a slight angle, as shown in the diagram (above). When you are happy with the shape, trim the ends of the swag 1.5cm outside the lines of gathering stitches. Open out the pattern and mark the lines of gathering stitch with dressmaker's chalk.

6 *Make pattern for the tails △*
Cut a piece of fabric for each tail, omitting seam allowances, and cutting the lower edge on the bias. Hang them in place and adjust the folds, then staple the pattern to the top of the pelmet, so you can check the effect. Mark the pleat lines (shown in blue), the fold for the return and the line of the top of the pelmet shelf (shown here in red).

7 Make adjustments to calculations
Use the fabric patterns to check exactly how much fabric you need. Make sure you have included an allowance of 1.5cm for seams all round and include an allowance for matching patterns if this is necessary.

MAKING THE SWAGS

Use the pattern you made from lining fabric as a guide when making up the swags. Unpick the gathering stitches at one end, so you can use the pattern as a guide to both cutting and gathering the fabric for the swag.

1 Cut out fabric and lining
Using your pattern as a guide, and adding 1.5cm seam allowance all round, cut out the swag in both fabric and lining (or contrast fabric).

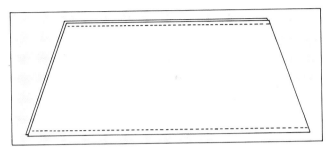
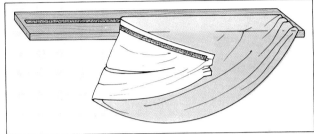

2 Make up the swag △
Lay the two pieces of fabric on top of each other with right sides together. Pin, tack and stitch together along top and bottom edges, leaving the ends open. Press and trim seam allowances. Turn right side out and press.

3 Gather the ends
Gather or pleat the ends of the swags to match the pattern you made. Temporarily staple the fabric to the top of the pelmet shelf to check the effect. Take down the swag, and, if you are happy with the gathers, trim the raw edges and bind along the gathered edge to give a neat finish.

4 Fit the Velcro △
Stitch the hooked half of a strip of Velcro to the top edge of the swag, and staple the other half to the top of the pelmet shelf. (If you do not want to take down the swag for cleaning, you can staple or tack it directly in place along the top edge.)

MAKING THE TAILS

The tails are made up using the pattern you have already cut, like the swags. Start with the pattern piece opened out flat, with the fold lines and pelmet positions marked on it, as shown in step 6 on the opposite page.

1 Check the pattern pieces
Check that the patterns for the tails are exact mirror images, and adjust slightly if necessary. Cut out a pair of tails in fabric and lining, including a 1.5cm seam allowance all round. Transfer the fold lines and the line marking the corner of the pelmet shelf (where appropriate) to the tails.

2 Make up the tails
Position the panels of fabric for each tail on top of each other, right sides facing, and stitch together down sides and across lower edge, leaving top edge open. Press, trim seam allowances and clip corners and turn right side out. Press.

BRIGHT IDEA

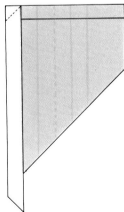
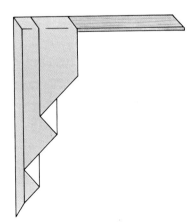

3 Make pleats △
If the tails are to go around the return of the pelmet shelf, fold the tail back on itself, right sides together, along the marked corner line. Make a diagonal row of stitching through both layers of fabric (like a dart) from the outer corner of the pelmet shelf to the top corner of the tail. This will give you a neat box shape at the top of the tail. Pleat the fabric along the marked lines and tack together across the top.

4 Finish top edge △
Check the fit by hanging in place. Press. Trim the top edge if necessary, and bind or oversew raw edges.

5 Attach Velcro
Stitch one half of the Velcro to the underside of the top of the tails, and attach the other half to the top of the shelf. Hang in place, then add extra tabs of Velcro if necessary where the swags and tails overlap, to hold them together.

Swathed in lace For instant effect with a minimum of sewing, you can simply drape a length of lace over a wooden pole above the window. Just measure the length from the floor to the top of the pole, double it, and add an allowance for a generous sweep of fabric. Velcro can be used to anchor the drape in place

COUNTRY-STYLE SWAG

For cottage-style windows, you can make swags and tails on a simpler scale from a single length of fabric, fixed at each end to a batten above the window. If the curtains are fitted in a recess, a 50 × 12.5mm batten is sufficient. If the curtains have to be hung outside the recess, fit a 50 × 32mm batten, and fit the curtain track to the underside of the batten.

1 *Measure up the window* ▷
Measure the batten above the window and decide how far down you want the swag to fall, and how long the tails should be. The easiest way to measure is to loop a tape measure where the swag is to be hung. Alternatively, hold a piece of string or strip of fabric in place, check the effect and then measure that to see how much fabric you will need for the swag.

2 *Calculate amount of fabric* ▷ ▷
For a neat effect, it is best to shape the ends, and make the gathering stitches at an angle. You can use lining fabric or old sheeting to made a pattern, marking the lines of gathering with dressmaker's chalk. The length is the length calculated in step 1. The width should be about 1½ times the depth of the swag. Include an allowance for neatening the edges of the drape (see below).

3 *Cut out the fabric*
Use the pattern to cut out fabric for the swag. The edges may be bound, in which case you will not need to add an allowance for neatening, or you can turn under a 1cm double hem all round the edge of the panel. A third alternative is to line the panel, in which case you should include a 1.5cm seam allowance, and cut a matching panel in lining fabric or some other toning fabric to the same measurements.

4 *Neaten edges of panel*
Bind or hem raw edges, or line the panel by stitching the lining to the panel, right sides facing, stitching all round the edge, leaving a 10cm gap: turn to right side and close opening.

5 *Gather corners*
Fold the panel in half, right sides together. Mark the points where the swag is to be gathered, to match the fixing points at the ends of the batten above the window. Make two lines of gathering stitches at each point. Draw up the gathers. Stitch the gathers to a piece of tape at the back of the swag.

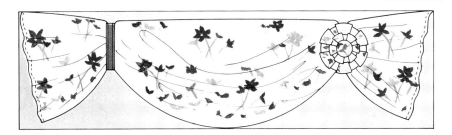

6 *Neaten the front* △
Use lengths of ribbon or a rosette or bow made from matching fabric to cover the lines of gathering stitches. A neat tab gives a more tailored effect.

7 *Hang the swag*
Hang the swag at the window, either by screwing small cup hooks to the batten, and curtain rings to the back of the gathers, or with a length of Velcro fixed to the top of the swag and the batten.

▷ *Simple swag*
This small window has been dressed with unlined curtains, with standard headings. A simple swag across the top covers the curtain track and adds a country feeling in a teenage bedroom.

CHOOSING CURTAINS

An appealing window treatment immediately attracts attention and transforms and enhances any room.

This chapter covers simple curtain treatments to help you choose the right style to suit your furnishings. Later chapters cover curtain tracks and poles and various types of blinds so that you can plan your window treatments.

The style of the curtains should complement the decor as well as the shape of the window. Do you want the curtains to look informal or rather 'dressy', tailored or romantic, modern or of a particular period? Decide whether you want the curtains to stand out or blend with the furnishings. If there is a spectacular view, keep the curtains simple. If the view is unattractive you can disguise it with a permanent curtain made from a sheer fabric or, if daylight is not important, choose curtains that are fixed at the top and held back at the sides.

Lined or unlined? As a rule, lining makes a curtain look and hang better, as well as adding insulation and protecting the curtain fabric from fading. Thermal linings and interlinings both help insulate against cold.

Unlined curtains, however, do have a place. Lightweight fabrics, laces and sheers filter the light attractively, and can be teamed with a blind for night-time privacy.

Fabrics for curtains It is usually better to be generous with a cheaper fabric than mean with an expensive one. Buy a short length of your chosen fabric to take home so you can check how it drapes and see how it looks with the rest of your furnishings, and in different lights. (You can use it to make tiebacks or a cushion cover later on.)

HOW LONG?

Sill-length curtains work well in cottagey rooms or with horizontal windows in modern homes. Curtains should barely touch the sill.

Below-sill length can look untidy when drawn back but if you have a radiator under the window you can finish the curtains just above it.

Floor-length curtains work best with sash windows, in bays and bows and, of course, french and picture windows. The curtains should almost touch the floor with no visible gap.

Café curtains give privacy at the lower half of a window while letting in light at the top.

  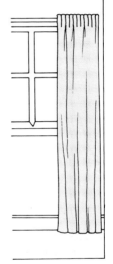 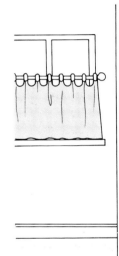

CURTAIN STYLE

STRAIGHT CURTAINS
Style Suitable for long or short curtains in modern and most traditional rooms.
In use Hang from a track or pole, with or without pelmet or valance.

TIEBACKS
Style Used to hold curtains back in an elegant curve to give a softer, fuller look.
In use Curtains can be left touching at the centre and looped back, or half drawn and looped back, depending on light.
Watchpoints Don't pull curtains into a straight line, but ease them into a curve. Not recommended for velvet.

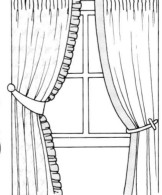

CURTAIN TRIMMINGS
Style A decorative edge gives a curtain a lot of extra style. A narrow frill looks pretty; a plain co-ordinated border is more tailored.

CHECKLIST
To help you decide what kind of curtains you want, here is a quick checklist of points to consider.

- ☐ What shape and size is the window?
- ☐ What look do you want to achieve?
- ☐ How long do you want the curtains to be?
- ☐ What heading?
- ☐ Lined or unlined?
- ☐ Hung from a pole or track?
- ☐ With or without a pelmet or valance?
- ☐ To hang straight, to curve with tiebacks?
- ☐ Combined with a sheer/net curtain or blind?
- ☐ What is the main function – privacy, insulation, light exclusion?
- ☐ Will frequent cleaning be necessary?

TYPES OF HEADINGS

A ready-made curtain heading tape is the easiest way of creating a decorative effect for both curtains and valances.

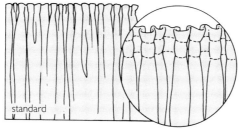
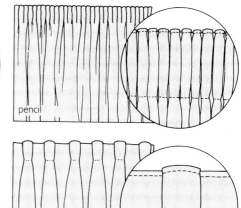

STANDARD HEADING
Style Suitable for sheers and informal, lightweight, sill-length curtains.
In use Gives an evenly gathered, narrow heading. A synthetic tape is available for sheers and nets.
Watchpoint Curtains can look unfinished without a pelmet or valance when drawn back.

PENCIL PLEATING
Style This neat, unobtrusive heading suits most furnishing styles, particularly rooms with a modern look.
In use Tape comes in two widths: narrow for short curtains, deep for longer ones. The tape forms neat pleats, and is suitable for lined and unlined curtains in a medium-weight fabric. The curtain can be hung from rings or hooked to stand up in front of the track and so does not need a pelmet or valance.

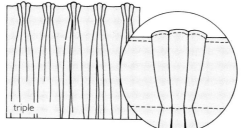

TRIPLE PLEATING
Style This heading looks well on long curtains and suits more traditional styles of furnishing. The regular, full folds look good in velvet.
In use The tape forms spaced pleats which can be straight or fanned out. It is suitable for medium- to heavyweight fabrics and can be hung from rings or to cover the track.
Watchpoint Position the tape so that the pleats fall evenly across the curtains with equal space at each end.

CARTRIDGE PLEATING
Style A formal heading, especially suitable for heavier, floor-length curtains in an elegant setting. Again, good for velvet.
Watchpoint Position the tape so that the single pleats fall evenly across the curtain.

PELMETS AND VALANCES

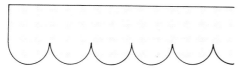
straight pelmet

valance

shaped pelmet

frilled valance

A pelmet or valance hides the curtain track and heading and adds a decorative touch to a window.

STRAIGHT PELMET
Style The simple clean lines suit a formal or modern setting. The depth and width can alter the proportions of the window.
In use You can paint or paper the pelmet to match the walls.
Watchpoint Make sure the pelmet projects sufficiently to clear the curtains.

SHAPED PELMET
Style Choose a decorative edge – scalloped, curved, castellated, etc – to suit a more elaborate style of furnishing.
In use The stiffened pelmet backing is pre-printed with a variety of shapes: simply remove the adhesive backing and cover with the fabric of your choice.
Watchpoint Fabric-covered pelmets are difficult to clean, so do not use them in rooms such as kitchens and bathrooms.

VALANCE
Style The depth of a valance varies according to the size of the window and style of curtain. Short curtains need a minimum of 75mm/3in; long curtains can take a valance as deep as 30cm/12in. Simple valances look best in informal, cottagey rooms.
In use Valances fix to a pelmet shelf or hang from a valance track. Use a heading tape that matches the curtains below.

FRILLED VALANCE
Style For a more decorative look the bottom edge of a valance can have a frill added. It can also be ruched like a festoon blind, swagged or curved so that it is deeper at the sides.
Watchpoint The depth of the curve must be in proportion to the length of the curtain.

MORE CURTAIN IDEAS

These simple ideas for windows are mainly suitable for sheer or lightweight fabrics and do not use any complicated curtain-making techniques.

Cross-over curtains made from lace or voile look pretty and romantic. A length of bordered cotton lace is draped over a pole and looped back at the sides by rosette brackets. Sew hems at each end to neaten and team with a roller blind for privacy.

A draped fabric curtain made from a length of lightweight furnishing fabric adds an elegant finish to a more formal room. One end of the fabric is wrapped around the pole (staple or use Velcro to hold it if necessary), and the fabric is then arranged in a deep swag across the window and down one side. An elegant roman blind will complement this style as well as giving privacy at night.

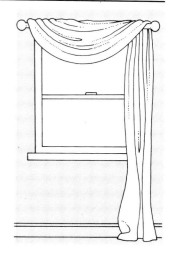

CHOOSING FABRIC FOR CURTAINS

Whatever curtains you want, there is a fabric for the job – finding it is just a matter of knowing what to look for.

There's more to shopping for curtain fabric than seeking out the perfect print or the weave that complements the colour scheme to perfection. Furnishing fabrics are not all suitable for every situation. With the wide range of weaves and weights of cloth available, make sure the one you buy will do the job you have in mind.

The two most important factors to bear in mind when looking for curtain fabric are resistance to fading and the weight of the fabric.

Light resistance Curtains, being so close to windows, take a lot of punishment from sunlight. Make sure to choose fabrics that are resistant to fading and rotting by the sun's rays, particularly for rooms which get the sun throughout most of the day. If the fabric you choose is subject to fading – a dupion for instance – line it with curtain lining fabric or add some form of sunscreen such as sheer curtains or plain roller blinds.

Fabric weights Look at the weight and quality of the fabric. In general, all but the lightest curtains are worth lining, and even some of the thinner softer cloths which drape well look very limp unless they are lined. It is worth taking trouble to line or interline an expensive fabric – this will enhance the appearance of the fabric and also help to insulate your room.

Heavyweight curtain fabrics are best made up into full-length curtains, as they can look stiff and bulky when made up into sill-length curtains.

Making the right choice When you have decided what curtain fabric you want, it is worth investing in a metre to bring home. This way you can check colour and pattern against the existing furnishings and see how the fabric reacts both to the natural and the artificial light in the room. The extra expense is worthwhile to make sure you have made the right choice, and to avoid making an expensive mistake. The odd length of fabric can always be made into covers for scatter cushions.

Before the fabric is cut for you in the shop, check that there are no flaws in the weave. If it is a print, make sure that the pattern is printed square on the fabric – if you are joining widths to make up the curtain and the pattern is printed off the grain by more than a couple of centimetres, you will not be able to match the pattern without distorting the fall of the cloth.

FABRIC FIBRES

Acetate	A synthetic silky-looking fibre often combined with cotton or linen in brocades and open weave effects. Usually washable and non-shrinking.
Acrylic	A synthetic fibre used for lightweight but strong and crease-resistant fabrics and also for velvets and satins. Does not fade and is washable, but on no account should it be boiled as this harms the fibre.
Cotton	A strong and hardwearing natural fibre which becomes stronger when it is wet, so it can be rubbed, scrubbed and boiled during washing. It is very absorbent and so takes dyes and printing well. Cotton is inclined to shrink when first washed unless it has been pre-shrunk by the manufacturer. So before making up, shrink cotton materials by damping or immersing them in water. All types of cotton are suitable for curtains.
Fibreglass	A synthetic flame-resistant fibre which makes full drapes. Dry clean.
Hessian	A natural fibre made from jute or hemp, available in a wide range of colours. Prone to fading. Dry clean.
Linen	A natural fibre made from flax; stronger than cotton. Used to make a variety of fabrics from strong linen cloth to fine lawn.
Milium	A synthetic fibre used for aluminium-backed curtain linings with good insulation properties. Dry clean.
Nylon	A synthetic fibre used for fabrics of all weights and types. Varieties include nylon velvet and nets. Shrink-resistant, washable, but can fade.
Polyester	A very strong synthetic fibre often blended with natural fibres. Does not shrink or fade. Popular for its sheer and opaque qualities.
Rayon	A synthetic fibre originally known as artificial silk. Includes taffeta, linen types and velvet. Tends to fray. Follow manufacturer's instructions.
Silk	A natural fibre produced by the silkworm. It has always been a luxury furnishing fabric and traditionally, all velvets, taffetas, moirés and damasks were made of it. Pure silk curtains always need to be lined and interlined to give the weight and substance required. It will fade and rot in sunlight, but shouldn't shrink if washed with care. Dry clean or hand wash according to manufacturer's instructions.
Wool	A natural fibre which is crease and soil-resistant and dyes well. If not pre-shrunk, fabric will shrink. Follow manufacturer's instructions.

Most manufacturers disclaim responsibility for faults once the fabric has been cut, so it is important to make sure that there are no faults in the fabric before picking up your scissors.

Fabric care The after-care of made-up curtains also needs some thought when choosing fabric. Unless a fabric is labelled and sold as pre-shrunk or fixed-finished, a shrinkage of between five and six per cent is considered normal,

and even after pre-shrinking, a fabric can still shrink by up to three per cent.

It is always recommended that lined curtains should be dry cleaned. This is because the various components, the fabric, the lining and the thread, as well as the cord and tape, do not necessarily shrink at the same rate.

If curtains are going to need regular washing it is sensible either to pre-wash the fabric, lining and tape, or to make

curtains with detachable linings.

Full-length curtains, where the shrinkage potential will be more noticeable, should have generous hems, loosely stitched in case they need to be let down later on. (It is advisable to undo the stitching before washing for the first time.)

Remember the 'true' length of a curtain should be the drop it has to cover plus allowances for hem and heading.

FABRIC WEAVES AND FINISHES

The characteristics of the fibres in a fabric determine how well the fabric hangs, washes and wears.

△ BROCADE

This is a woven fabric with a raised floral design that looks like embroidery. It can be made from silk, linen or cotton, or from synthetic yarn.

△ CALICO

This is an unbleached plain woven cotton of medium weight in a matt finish, available in natural off-white. It is relatively cheap and must be used lavishly to look effective. It looks good draped into dramatic window treatments. It is a strong firmly woven fabric, which washes well although it tends to crease and shrink, so wash with care.

COTTON SATIN

This is a less expensive and more practical alternative to satin (which was traditionally made from pure silk). It is a hard wearing, very close weave with a distinctive sheen. A heavy-quality version makes luxuriously soft and natural curtains that drape extremely well. It adds a sophisticated finish to curtains in the more formal rooms of your home.

Cotton satin is often used as the base cloth for printing, but is also popular as a plain self-coloured weave. Sometimes a minor design, such as a spot or small diamond, is introduced as surface decoration.

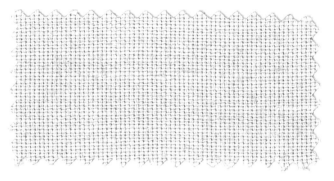

△ COTTON LINEN OR LINEN UNION

This is a blend of cotton and linen to which small quantities of nylon are added for strength. When made up into heavy full lengths it drapes reasonably well, but is really too stiff for short curtains.

Wash at a maximum of 40 °C; the two fibres do not shrink evenly at higher temperatures.

△ DAMASK

This was originally made in silk but now comes in cotton and various natural/synthetic blends. Its weave produces patterns which appear matt against a shiny, satin-like background.

△ DUPION

This fabric mimics silk, but is much cheaper. Sometimes it is heavily slubbed (woven with alternate thick and thin threads) to resemble raw silk. It is usually woven in synthetic fibres, often on an acetate warp (lengthwise threads.) There are a few washable versions available in viscose/cotton or acrylic/linen blends, but it usually has to be dry cleaned. Dupion is a lightweight cloth that needs lining and preferably inter lining, but it drapes well and can be made up successfully into short and full-length curtains.

As with pure silk, problems can arise with fading, especially with stronger and brighter colourways.

EASYCARE COTTON
This is a cotton which has been treated to a polished finish which gives a soft and silky touch to the surface of the cloth. The easy-care finish means the fabric drapes and washes beautifully.

GINGHAM
A lightweight cotton fabric or poly/cotton with a checked pattern woven in using two coloured yarns.

△ GLAZED COTTON OR CHINTZ
This has an attractive shiny finish which suits prints intended for curtains in more formal rooms, although it is available in plains as well as prints. The glazing can be light, giving a soft sheen, or high for a bright, crisp effect; it is applied only to 100 per cent cotton. The cloth is usually lightweight but tightly woven, so it accepts dyes and glaze well.

Glazed cotton is often called chintz after the early Indian-inspired chintz prints which were finished in this way.

It can be dry cleaned or hand washed. The fabric should not be rubbed and should be kept as flat as possible in the water. Iron while damp.

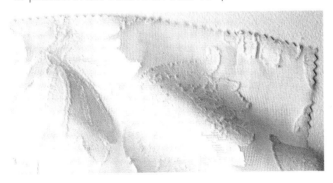

△ LACE AND MADRAS
These are attractive alternatives to voiles and sheers. Lace was originally made from linen and the fine open work patterns were hand-made. These days most laces are machine-made from cotton, nylon or viscose. Although quality and care depend on whether natural or synthetic yarns are used, cotton lace and fine madras can be washed with care and starched for a crisp finish.

△ MUSLIN
A fine, loosely-woven cotton, ideal for sheer curtains.

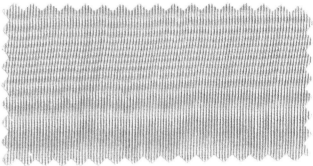

△ MOIRÉ
Also known as watered silk, this is now usually made from synthetic fibres. The distinctive, light-reflecting, wavy pattern is applied by machine to a plain, lightly ribbed cloth. To preserve the pattern, fabric should be dry cleaned. It makes elegant curtains, suited to formal rooms. Moiré fabrics are available in plain colours and in stripes, and occasionally over-printed with a traditional design.

Moiré can react to changes of temperature and humidity in a room. It absorbs and releases moisture, shrinking and expanding like wood, so it should be sewn with as loose a tension as possible to allow for this potential movement in the cloth.

△ POLYESTER COTTON
As its name implies, this is a blend of cotton and the synthetic fibre, polyester. Although usually associated with bedlinen, some curtain prints are made in this fabric. Many printed polyester cotton bed sheets can also be made up into light and inexpensive curtains, which wash well and withstand strong sunlight with only minimal fading.

It is an easy-care fabric – strong and durable, reasonably crease-resistant and keeps its shape. When putting fabrics of blended fibres such as polyester cotton in a washing machine, programme the machine according to the most delicate fibre in the blend.

draping qualities of cotton velour and do not make good short curtains.

The pile can lie either up or down but make sure that the same direction is maintained throughout. If the pile runs upwards the colour is usually richer than when it runs downwards. Take care not to crush the pile when making-up; any pressure marks should steam out. Once curtains have been hanging for a few weeks any marks made while making up should disappear.

△ PRINTED COTTON

This offers the widest choice of patterns and designs in a large variety of colours. It makes up well and the dyes are generally colourfast. Price variation reflects the quality of the base cloth, the exclusiveness of the design and the number of colours used.

SATEEN

A lightweight fabric, used mainly for curtain linings, although heavier weights may be used for curtains. Similar to satin, it is generally made of cotton.

△ SEERSUCKER

The characteristic appearance – puckered and flat stripy effect – is achieved by a heat process in manufacture or by grouping the lengthwise threads alternatively tight and loose when weaving. It is ideal for light, airy, unlined curtains, is usually made of cotton and is washable.

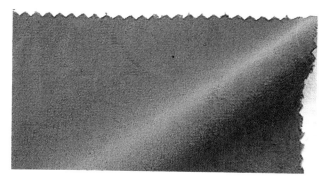

△ VELVETS

With the exception of silk, which is very expensive, cotton velour is the best quality velvet to use. It drapes softly even though the fabric is heavy and makes up into good short as well as long curtains. Dyes are generally good and shouldn't fade. Velvets can be crushed for effect or cut to form patterns.

Acrylic velvet, often called Dralon, (the brand name of the major manufacturer of acrylic fibre) is an upholstery cloth, but the lighter qualities can be made into curtains. However, they do not have the good

△ VOILES AND SHEERS

These are usually made from synthetic fibres such as nylon and polyester and can be hand or machine washed with virtually no shrinkage. They are made from closely woven yarns, which give a flimsy, fluid effect.

Some voiles co-ordinate with printed cottons so that the same outline or motif is repeated on both fabrics. They are also available in a plain weave.

Voiles and sheers are often used to give privacy to rooms which are overlooked and also help to filter strong sunlight and protect furnishings and curtains from fading.

CHOOSING FABRICS FOR BLINDS

Here are some guidelines to help you make the right choice when it comes to selecting fabrics suitable for blind making.

Roller blinds Fabric needs to be flexible enough to roll around a wooden dowel. All medium-weight fabrics can be used, but look for tightly woven cottons for really reliable results. Fabric should be treated with a stiffener, but allow for slight shrinkage from this process. Use flame resistant and wipe-down fabrics for kitchen or bathroom blinds.

Roman blinds give a tailored yet elegant look. Use cotton prints or any closely woven fabric of medium weight. Do not treat fabric with a stiffening agent as this stops it falling into natural folds.

Austrian blinds are made from light or medium weight fabrics which hang well and look good when gathered into swags. For best results they should be lined. They can be trimmed with a ruffle or length of lace or madras. A lining fabric might also be necessary.

Festoon blinds use much more fabric than austrian blinds. Soft, lightweight and delicate fabrics which allow the light to filter through are most suited to the permanent ruched swags.

CURTAIN TRACKS AND POLES

The choice between hanging your curtains on a track or a pole depends to a certain extent on the look you wish to achieve.

Poles are usually chosen for the more traditional style of furnishing or where the curtains feature as a focal point in a room. They are particularly suitable for long straight runs and heavy floor-length curtains, and look better than tracks for curtains without valances or pelmets. Wooden poles can be mitred at corners to fit bow windows, but they cannot be used on curved bays.

Pole kits are sold complete with brackets, rings and pole ends. It is also possible to buy these items separately, so you can make up a set to suit your particular requirements or add brackets or rings to a kit.

Tracks have a streamlined look suitable for most modern furnishing styles and are generally cheaper than poles. The curtains are hooked on to runners designed to glide smoothly along the track. Lightweight plastic and aluminium tracks can be bent to fit bow and bay windows and steel tracks are available for the heaviest of curtains.

Tracks are sold with fittings to fix them to the wall or ceiling and with or without runners, end stops or cross-over arms (see over). Runners are made from plastic or brass and vary in style to fit a particular track. If the track doesn't have a cord pulley, an end stop needs to be fixed at each end to prevent the runners from falling off.

Cording Although some poles and tracks have integral cording, cording sets can be added to most types so that the curtains can be drawn without handling the fabric.

Wire and rods are the simplest supports for lightweight curtains. Thread them through a casing and use them in small windows or across a recess.

POSITIONING THE POLE OR TRACK

A pole or track can be fixed within the window recess if it is a deep one, or if a bay or bow, on the window frame itself or outside and above it.

The placing of the pole or track can make the window look larger or smaller. For example, the pole can be extended well beyond the frame (right), so that the curtain can be pulled clear of the window, letting in the maximum amount of light and making a small window seem wider.

A pair of curtains fixed together across the top of a window and held back at the sides (far right) will reduce the height of a very tall window.

A concealed track placed along the top of the window makes an unobtrusive curtain fitment which can be painted or papered to match the paintwork or wallpaper.

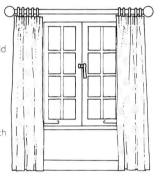

WOODEN POLES

Style Plain varnished poles fit a traditional or country setting while painted poles suit a modern or informal style. The pole ends can be simple or elaborately turned to suit the furnishing style.

In use Cording sets can be added to the wider diameter poles.

Watchpoint Allow sufficient diameter poles and brackets to support the weight of curtain and width of the window.

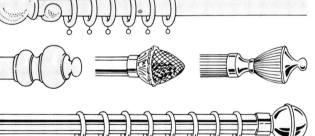

BRASS POLES

Style Brass or brass-finished metal poles suit a more formal style of furnishing. The pole finish can be reeded with elaborate pole ends for elegant curtains or plain with simple ends for a modern setting.

In use Some poles have internal cording sets to draw curtains on concealed runners instead of rings. Ring-based cording sets can be added to wider diameter poles. Some poles adjust telescopically.

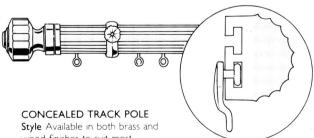

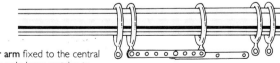

Cross-over arm fixed to the central rings allows pole-hung curtains to overlap at the centre.

CONCEALED TRACK POLE

Style Available in both brass and wood finishes to suit most traditional furnishing styles. The fake finish looks best seen at a distance, so use the poles over tall windows or at ceiling height.

In use The semicircular pole conceals the track system which is combined with a cording set.

Watchpoint The track is less rigid than a solid wood or brass pole so several mountings may be needed to support it, according to the width of the window.

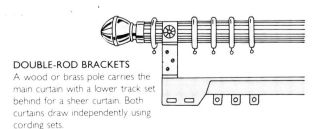

DOUBLE-ROD BRACKETS

A wood or brass pole carries the main curtain with a lower track set behind for a sheer curtain. Both curtains draw independently using cording sets.

CURTAIN TRACKS

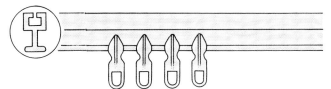

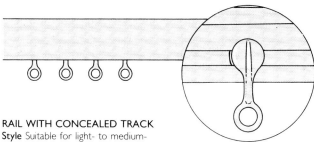

BASIC TRACK
Style Lightweight plastic or aluminium track, with or without a cross-over arm, is suitable for light- to medium-weight fabrics and sheers.

In use Can be fitted within a recess, on the frame, or above it if frame is flush to the wall. It comes in different lengths and is cut to fit. Is best used under a pelmet or valance.

RAIL WITH CONCEALED TRACK
Style Suitable for light- to medium-weight fabrics. Track can be left plain or papered to match wall. It is also available with a reeded gold trim.
In use Available with or without internal cording and cross-over arms and fixed at intervals, depending on the weight of the curtains. Comes in different lengths and is cut to fit. The plastic track can be bent by hand to fit round bays or bow windows. Aluminium track is bent professionally when ordered.

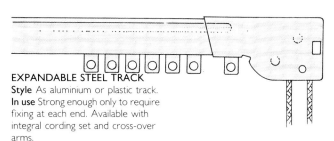

EXPANDABLE STEEL TRACK
Style As aluminium or plastic track.
In use Strong enough only to require fixing at each end. Available with integral cording set and cross-over arms.

CEILING MOUNTED TRACK
Style Available in two styles. A narrow, neat plastic track that can be fitted to the underside of a window or recessed into plaster; it is suitable for lightweight curtains and is ideal for small windows. Or a wider track with a pulley housing at one end for the cording, suitable for medium-weight fabrics.
In use The simpler types of heading tape are best.

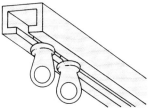

Watchpoint The track needs to be well fixed to the ceiling.

TRACK WITH DOUBLE HOOKS
Style Made from plastic or aluminium and can be bent to fit into the most awkward of bay windows.
In use The double hooks are detachable and simply clip on to the face of the track; they are designed to carry curtains with separate linings. Cording sets are available for straight runs.

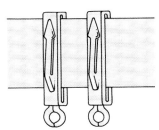

COMBINED TRACK AND VALANCE RAIL
Style The plastic track/rail can be bent by hand; the aluminium track needs to be bent professionally.
In use The curtain hangs from the track and draws in the normal way, while the valance hooks simply clip over the rail.
Watchpoint Match the valance and curtain heading tapes.

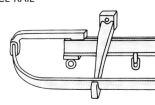

CURTAIN WIRE AND RODS

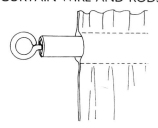

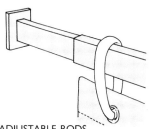

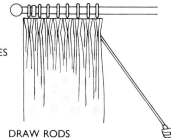

DOWEL RODS AND METAL TUBES
They fit into metal sockets screwed into a reveal or recess and make a strong, more permanent rail. Suitable for heavier curtains.

PLASTIC-COVERED EXPANDABLE WIRE
Hooks on each end of the wire clip into fixed screw eyes. Use with lightweight or sheer fabrics with a casing at the top or at both top and bottom.

ADJUSTABLE RODS
These have a telescopic spring fixing which grips inside a reveal or window recess. Sizes range from 40-185cm. Use for light- to medium-weight fabrics with a cased heading or with rings for a shower curtain.

SWIVEL RODS
Fixed to a bracket at one end, these are ideal for curtains that need to be swung back out of the way, such as at dormer windows.

DRAW RODS
These are attached to the leading ring at the centre front of pole-hung curtains, making them easy to draw – repeated drawing by hand marks the curtains and drags at the pole and rings. When not in use the rods hang at the back, hidden by the folds.

SUPPORTING LONG POLES AND TRACKS

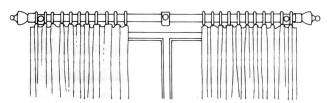

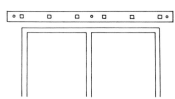

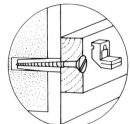

Choose the wider diameter poles for long runs over wide picture windows and for floor-length curtains in heavy fabrics. Prevent sagging by adding one or two extra brackets (position them so they won't affect the drawing of the curtains).

Tracks need brackets along their length to support any but the lightest fabrics.
Many windows have a concrete lintel above the frame, so to avoid drilling for several mountings, it is better to screw a batten into the lintel and mount the brackets on this. The batten can be either painted or papered to match the wall covering.

DEALING WITH PROBLEM WINDOWS

Oddly shaped, very small or very large windows can be difficult to fit with curtains.

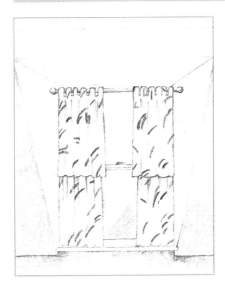

△ *Deep dormers*
Two layers of café curtains are a good way to treat deep dormers – and to adapt curtains which are too short for other use.

ATTIC IDEAS

Problem Sloping roof lights and attic windows set into a deep dormer can be difficult to curtain without cutting off natural light.

Solution If you are fitting new sloping rooflights, look for the type with a blind sandwiched between two layers of glass. Special venetian blinds are available for existing windows. They don't drop forward and can be adjusted to any angle to restrict or admit light. Sheer curtains or lace panels can be held at the top and bottom of the frame with a brass or wooden rod.

Deep dormer windows let in less light than sloping windows. If the window is not overlooked, fit a simple café curtain. If it is, fit a second set of short curtains fitted at the top (see above). This is a good way to make use of curtains which are too short or narrow for other windows in the house. Simply cut them in half, hem the bottom of the top pieces and add a heading to the bottom pieces.

Another way to treat this sort of window is to fit just one sheer curtain on a pole.

COPING WITH ARCHES

Problem Hanging a conventional curtain track at arched windows spoils the shape of the arch and the proportions of the windows.

Solution Try to choose a treatment to flatter the shape of the windows. You can suspend a lace panel across the window just before it begins to curve, or fit curtains which clear the sides and the top of the arch when they are open. To do this, fit a curtain track about 10cm (4in) above the arch of the window and about 7.5cm (3in) wider than the window at each side.

For a classic look, fit shutters the same length as the window (measured from the centre of the arch to the bottom). The shutters can be kept open during the day and closed at night.

It is possible to fit a track, pelmet and curtains to follow the shape of the arch (see below) but this is a job for a professional curtain maker and fitter as the track must be specially bent and the fabric cut on a curve.

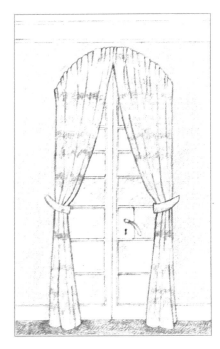

△ *Professional treatment*
This sort of treatment makes the most of an arched window but needs the skills of a professional to make and fit curtains.

△ *Three-way bay*
Roller blinds are a simple, effective way to cover a bay made up of three large windows.

THREE WINDOW BAYS

Problem In many homes, the main window at the front of the house is a bay made up of three large windows, sometimes with a space between each one.

Solution Curtains for bay windows should clear the window during the day, not divide it up. Hang the curtains on a track which bends so that the curtains follow the shape of the bay. A corded track is best – wide, heavy curtains are difficult to pull by hand. If the bay is overlooked, hang sheer blinds for daytime use. The curtains and blinds can be combined with a matching pelmet.

If you want a simple, unfussy treatment, hang roller, roman, venetian, slatted wood or straw blinds at each window, (see above).

LEADED LIGHT CASEMENTS

Problem Small, leaded light (diamond or square pane) casements are difficult to curtain without cutting off nearly all the natural light.

Solution Keep the curtains short on leaded light windows. Mount them on a pole, or add a crispy pleated valance. Position the track about 7.5cm (3in) above the frame and make it about 7.5cm (3in) longer at each side so that the curtains clear the window during the day and let in the maximum amount of natural light. Tiebacks can be used to hold the curtains away from the window when they are drawn back.

It is important to consider the size of the pattern on the curtain fabric in relation to the size of the window. Small casements look best hung with mini-print florals, small ginghams, candy stripes or plain fabric in a pale or subtle shade. Use a simple heading, such as triple pinch pleats. Don't use a bold design – it tends to look silly if only part of the pattern repeat covers the window or if the fabric has to be cut part of the way through a repeat.

△ *Top treatment*
An elaborately draped or swagged top makes tall, narrow windows seem much shorter and wider.

TREATMENTS FOR TALL WINDOWS

<u>Problem</u> A row of tall narrow windows look even longer and thinner when fitted with curtains hung from a conventional heading and track.

<u>Solution</u> Tall, narrow windows are usually sash type and are often in a row of two or three. The best way to make them look less long and thin is to fit an 'important' top treatment, such as a large, elaborate pelmet with 'tails' coming down over the curtains, a swathe of fabric wrapped around a pole (see above) or a pinch pleated or ruffled valance with floor-length curtains.

Alternatively, use a fabric with a strong horizontal pattern or with a deep border in a strong colour. Venetian blinds with shaded slats, starting with a light colour at the top, deepening to a dark tone at the bottom of the blind are a less fussy way to lower height.

ROOMS WITHOUT A VIEW

<u>Problem</u> An ugly or depressing view (such as a blank wall) can spoil the atmosphere of a room, but hiding it cuts out light as well as the scene outside.

<u>Solution</u> If the window is small (on a landing, for instance) and light isn't too important, hide the view with glass shelves filled with plants or a collection of coloured glass. Light from above to make a stunning display point. Where light is needed, fit a lace or sheer blind, or net café curtains over the bottom.

If the window looks out on to a blank wall, it may be possible to improve things by painting the wall white and training a climbing plant up it, or, if you are artistic, use vinyl emulsion to paint a pretty scene over the brickwork.

BATHROOM PRIVACY

<u>Problem</u> In many older houses, the bathroom is fitted into what was once a living area and has large, sash style windows fitted with clear glass.

<u>Solution</u> The obvious solution is to replace the panes with frosted glass but this does not look attractive from either inside or out. You can fit mirror glass so that you can see out but those outside can't see in – but this is expensive and available only from specialist glaziers. A lace blind is another simple solution, or a voile, lace or net café curtain can be fitted across the bottom half of the window.

Half shutters, either louvred and stained or painted or with the centre panel decorated to match the walls, are more inspiring (see below). They can be hinged, or fitted to a track so that they lift out for cleaning.

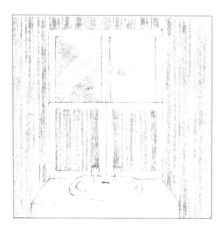

△ *Bathroom shutters*
Simple shutters are an unusual and attractive way to screen the bottom half of a big bathroom window.

AWKWARD WINDOWS

<u>Problem</u> When windows are positioned close to a fireplace, chimney breast, door or other obstruction, it is difficult to use two curtains.

<u>Solution</u> Austrian, roller or roman blinds solve the problem as they are pulled down from the top rather than from the sides. Use the same fabric as other curtains in the room, or choose a complementary plain colour. Plain blinds can be edged with a patterned fabric to match other curtains.

If you prefer curtains to blinds, hang just one curtain (see above right). The curtain should be one-and-a-half times as wide as the window so that it gathers at the top but still stretches from side to side. Hold the curtain back with a matching tieback or a piece of plaited fabric during the day. In a room where natural light is in short supply, the curtain can be made from a sheer fabric or from net.

△ *The single solution*
Where hanging two curtains is impossible, hang one extra wide curtain tied back at one side.

DEALING WITH PATIO DOORS

<u>Problem</u> Many homes have patio doors or french windows, often flanked by two smaller windows, which need a more interesting scheme than long curtains.

<u>Solution</u> Simple roller, roman or austrian blinds fitted to each window allow light in during the day and give privacy at night. If you want a more elaborate and decorative scheme, combine lace or voile blinds with long floor-to-ceiling curtains which can be pulled right across. During the day, the curtains can easily be held neatly in place against the side walls with matching or complementary tiebacks.

Where privacy during the day is important (if, for instance, the garden is overlooked) fit voile curtains to all three sections. They can be held at the top and bottom with a brass rod. In a high-tech room, slimline venetian or vertical blinds in grey or a cool pastel shade are a good choice.

THROUGH ROOMS

<u>Problem</u> 'Through' living rooms where two rooms have been joined often have a mixture of bay windows at one end and patio doors at the other.

<u>Solution</u> The first rule is to use the same style of curtains at each end of the room. As this type of room often looks long and narrow, try to use a bold, horizontal pattern on curtains at each end of the room. Make the curtains from floor to ceiling and preferably from wall to wall.

As an alternative, the patio doors can be fitted with roller blinds in a plain colour to complement or match curtain fabric. If the room has other small windows, fit them with plain blinds.

AUSTRIAN BLINDS

Austrian blinds – softly swagged and gathered – look impressively complicated but are easy to make.

These soft gathered blinds look good on their own, or can be used in addition to normal curtains or even simple roller blinds.

An austrian blind has a gathered or pencil-pleated curtain heading, and looks like an unlined curtain when completely lowered. The deep swags are made by pulling the fabric up by cords that are threaded through vertical rows of tape stitched to the back of the blind at regular intervals.

You can leave the blind plain, or add a frill to the bottom and side edges for an even softer effect.

Measuring up The blind is hung from a curtain track fixed to a wooden batten or from an austrian blind track. Fix the support temporarily in place so that exact measurements can be taken.

On a recessed window, fit the batten or track to the ceiling of the recess. If there is no recess, extend the batten or track 15cm beyond the edges of a plain window or flush with the outer edges of a moulded window frame.

Choosing fabric Choose a light fabric that drapes well so it gathers evenly across the blind. Suitable fabrics include moire, silk and voile, slubbed satin and soft cotton.

Types of tape For the vertical tape on the back of the blind, you can use a lightweight, narrow curtain heading tape with regular pockets so that rings can be attached for threading the cords.

Alternatively, use special austrian blind tape which has loops for holding the cords instead of rings.

To work out how much fabric and blind tape you need, see overleaf.

Ruffled charm
Austrian blinds work well in light fabrics that drape well. Here, peach-coloured seersucker is frilled and ruched into luxurious flounces.

CHECK YOUR NEEDS

To make the blind:
☐ Fabric
☐ Standard or pencil-pleat curtain heading tape to fit total fabric width
☐ Austrian blind tape or small plastic or metal curtain rings (split rings) and narrow heading tape with regular pockets to hold them
☐ Non-stretch cord
☐ Curtain hooks
☐ Cleat to tie the cords when blind is raised

☐ Sewing thread
☐ Tape measure
☐ Tailor's chalk
☐ Scissors
☐ Pins
☐ Needles
☐ Sewing machine
☐ Iron and ironing board

Note: Austrian blind kits can be bought from most department stores and include everything required for making a blind, apart from fabric and basic equipment listed above.

To mount the blind:
☐ Austrian blind track
  OR
☐ Wooden batten – 2.5cm thick, 5cm deep, and the same width as the window recess. If there's no recess, it should extend beyond the window
☐ Screw eyes to thread the cords through – you will need one screw eye for each vertical length of blind tape
☐ Curtain track of same width as the batten
☐ 2 angle irons (optional)

CALCULATING QUANTITIES

To calculate fabric needed, first fix the batten or track temporarily in place .

To get the width multiply the length of the battening or track by 2 times for standard gathered heading tape (by up to 2½ times for pencil-pleat tape – check manufacturer's instructions).

Divide this figure by the width of the fabric to give the number of fabric widths needed. Round up if necessary.

To get the length, measure from the top of the batten or track to the sill and add 45cm so that the lower edge of the blind is prettily swagged even when fully covering the window.

To get the total amount, multiply this figure by the number of fabric widths.
☐ If the fabric has a pattern repeat, add one full repeat per fabric width.
☐ To work out how much fabric you need for a frill, see page 56.

To get the amount of tape needed for the back of the blind, divide the total width of fabric into sections that are 20-40cm wide (see Step 3). You need sufficient tape to run from top to bottom of the blind along each vertical division and down both sides of the blind.

Cord for pulling up the blind – you need about double the amount of tape required (see Step 8).

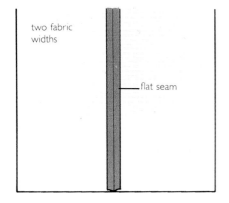

two fabric widths

flat seam

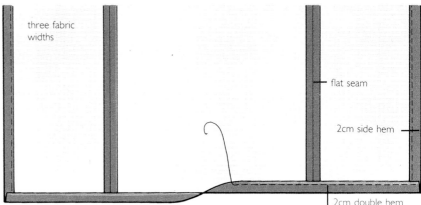

three fabric widths

flat seam

2cm side hem

2cm double hem

1 *Join fabric widths △*
For most windows you need to join at least two pieces of fabric to make up the width of the blind.

Use a simple flat seam and pin the widths together with right sides facing and any pattern matching. Tack and stitch 1.5cm from edges, then trim the seam allowance to 5mm. Remove tacking and press seam open.

Cut any surplus fabric evenly from both widths.

For three fabric widths *If you need to join three fabric widths to make up the width of the blind, position a complete width in the centre and add two equal pieces of fabric to the sides.*

2 *Hem the fabric △*
Down each side edge of the blind, turn a 2cm hem; pin and tack in place. Do not make this hem if you're adding side frills.

For a plain bottom edge, turn a double 2cm hem; pin, tack and stitch in place. Remove tacking and press.

Adding a frill *If you're adding a frill to bottom and/or side edges, do not hem fabric. Instead, make up frill and sew it in place (see page 56).*

3 *Mark positions of vertical tape*
Lay fabric, wrong side up, on the floor. Use tailor's chalk to mark vertical lines at regular intervals across the blind for the tape.

Mark the positions so that tapes cover the side hems and any joining seams in the fabric. Then mark vertical lines in between, spacing them evenly 20-40cm apart.

The size of the swag when fully drawn up will be about half the distance allowed between the tapes.

BRIGHT IDEA

Vertical guidelines
To make it easier to mark vertical lines across the blind, fold the fabric lengthways like a concertina every 20-40cm and press.

Open the fabric out again and you will have straight guidelines for positioning and attaching rows of tape.

7 Stitch rings in place ▽

Stitch the rings to the casing channels with one row down each side as shown and one or more rows down centre.

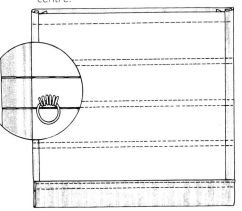

8 Cut up lengths of cord ▷

Decide which side of the blind you want the pull-up cord to hang. Lay the blind out flat, with the lining facing you. If you want the cords to hang down the left of the blind when it is hung, then with the wrong side of the blind facing you the cords should hang to the right of the blind (remember it is reversed). Cut the cord into appropriate lengths to run up the blind, across the top and down one side, allowing a little extra for knotting the cords.

Tie one end of each cord to a ring at the lower edge of the blind. Thread the cords up through the line of rings.

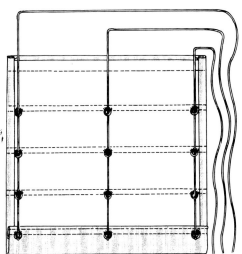

9 Prepare top batten

The batten is fitted with one narrow edge towards the window. Either drill holes in top batten to take suitable screws to fix the batten straight into the top of the window recess or attach angle irons to the underside of the batten so that it can be fitted to the wall or surround above the window.

Staple or tack the fabric to the batten so that the 5cm allowance lies over the top of the batten. Make sure the blind is absolutely straight.

10 Fit screw eyes ▷

Fit a screw eye into the batten at the top of each line of rings. Thread cords through the screw eyes, running them all to one side of the blind. Finish neatly by plaiting the ends of the cords and tie into an acorn.

11 Hang of blind

Either screw the batten straight into the top of the window recess, or fit angle irons above the window. Fix the cleat at one side to anchor cords.

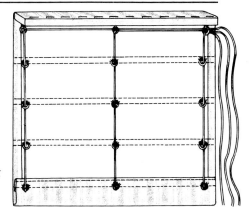

BRIGHT IDEA

NET EFFECTS

There's no reason why you shouldn't make roman blinds out of sheer fabric, to replace net curtains. Here, two layers of net have been used, with casings stitched to hold dowels as for lined blinds.

The two pieces of fabric should be cut 1.5cm larger down the sides and across the lower edge than the measurement of the finished blind, with an allowance of 5cm across the top as before. Join the two layers of fabric down the sides and across the lower edge, taking 1.5cm seams. Trim seam allowance and clip across corners. Turn right side out, and make up as for the lined blind, positioning the first casing about 10cm from lower edge. Space the casings about 20cm apart up the blind. Unpick the seam at one end of each casing. Slip dowels into the casings and then slipstitch the open end to hold the dowels in place. Note that only two rows of rings have been used, positioned close to the sides of the blind, so as to avoid clumsy cords running up the back of the blind.

TRIMS FOR ROMAN BLINDS

Because of the geometric styling of the blind a simple trim in plain braid or contrasting fabric is most effective.

1 *Braid trim across lower edge*
The simplest way to trim a roman blind is to add a length of braid across the lower edge. This looks particularly effective if it is attached close to the bottom of the blind so that it shows when the blind is pulled up. Allow a little extra fabric for turning at the bottom of the blind if you are using a wide braid, so that the bottom section of the blind hangs below the pleated section and the braid shows when the blind is pulled up. Stitch or glue the braid in place before inserting the lengths of dowel.

2 *Braid trim all round blind* ▷
Braid can be stitched in place down the side and across the lower edge of the blind, positioned a couple of centimetres in from the edge, with neatly mitred corners. Stitch the braid to the fabric before you start making up the blind: this will be easier if you use dressmaker's chalk to mark the finished edge 3cm from each side edge and 19cm from the lower edge of the fabric after cutting out. Decide on a suitable distance to space the braid from the edge of the blind (half to twice the width of the braid gives a good spacing, depending on that width). Then pin, tack and stitch the braid in place before joining the lining fabric and stitching the channels

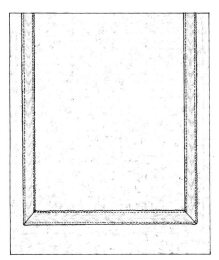

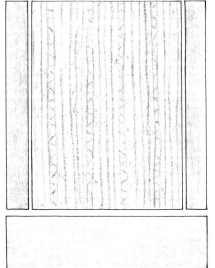

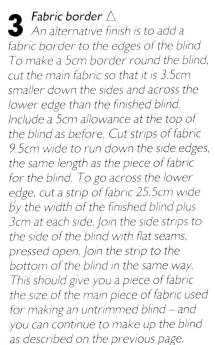

3 *Fabric border* △
An alternative finish is to add a fabric border to the edges of the blind To make a 5cm border round the blind, cut the main fabric so that it is 3.5cm smaller down the sides and across the lower edge than the finished blind. Include a 5cm allowance at the top of the blind as before. Cut strips of fabric 9.5cm wide to run down the side edges, the same length as the piece of fabric for the blind. To go across the lower edge, cut a strip of fabric 25.5cm wide by the width of the finished blind plus 3cm at each side. Join the side strips to the side of the blind with flat seams, pressed open. Join the strip to the bottom of the blind in the same way. This should give you a piece of fabric the size of the main piece of fabric used for making an untrimmed blind – and you can continue to make up the blind as described on the previous page.

◁ *Smartly pleated*
The neat, unfussy lines of roman blinds are well suited to modern, minimalist interior design. The blue-grey of the blind, neatly trimmed in clear red is echoed in the window seat, candlestick lamp and chaise longue.

BLINDS AND SHUTTERS

Choose a style which is neat and simple, elegantly swagged or slatted.

Blinds are a versatile way of covering windows. The styles range from the simple clean lines of a plain roller or venetian to the elegant swags of an austrian or festoon blind. Apart from these last two, most blinds have a contemporary feel but they can look at home in many traditional settings, particularly when used in combination with curtains.

Blinds are often the best answer if a window is awkwardly placed or space is limited and many of the simpler styles are cheaper than curtains.

Fabric blinds can be bought ready made or made to measure, or you can make many of the styles yourself using a simple kit following the instructions in this book.

Before you buy or make blinds, you must measure up accurately, using a steel tape measure.

The blinds can be fixed either within a recess or outside. For outside a recess allow an overlap of at least 4.5cm each side. If you are having blinds made to measure, always give the full width and drop dimensions of your finished blind – the manufacturer will make allowances for the fixing brackets.

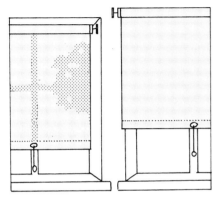

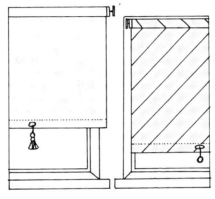

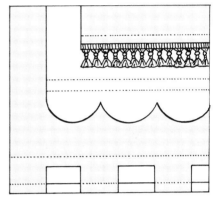

ROLLER BLINDS
Style One of the cheapest of window coverings, roller blinds can be bought ready made, made to measure or as a kit to make up yourself.
In use The fabric rolls round a wooden dowel by means of a spring-loaded mechanism or side pulley and the lower edge is weighted with a lath (thin strip of wood) inserted in a casing. Fabric choice can range from sheer net or voile to medium-weight furnishing fabrics. Waterproof or spongeable fabrics are ideal for bathrooms and kitchens and flame-retardant fabrics are also available.
Watchpoint Bulky weaves or materials with a pile are not suitable.

Border patterns are popular and there is also a wide choice of all-over pictorial prints, many of which are fun for a child's room. Dramatic geometric designs and bold diagonal patterns look particularly effective in a modern setting, while the softer floral or lacy net designs suit more traditional rooms.

The lower edge of a blind can be shaped to suit a more formal style of furnishing and lace, fringing, ribbon and braid add a decorative touch to both home-made or ready-made blinds. Blinds with a spring-loaded mechanism are raised or lowered by a cord which can be finished with the traditional wood acorn, tassel or ring.

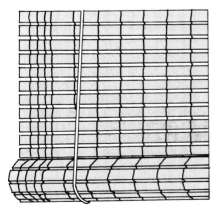

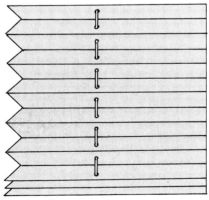

PINOLEUM BLINDS
Style Traditionally made from fine strips of wood woven together with cotton, today they are also made from plastic quills in a range of colours, including white. They filter the light attractively but can be seen through at night.
In use They roll up using a system of cords and pulleys and can be fixed at any level by winding the cord round a wall-fixed cleat.

PLEATEX BLINDS
Style Made from permanently pleated paper or polyester fabric. They are available in a range of attractive colours and sizes.
In use Raise and lower by using cords which pass through holes in the pleats. The fabric blinds can be treated with anti-static that repels dust, or can have a metallic backing to repel sun in summer and keep in warmth in winter.

CANE OR WOOD SLAT BLINDS
Style Cane blinds are made from split bamboo or rattan. Wood slats are strips of wood which are left natural or stained brown or different colours. Light filters through between the wood by day but they provide greater privacy than pinoleum blinds at night.
In use Bulkier than pinoleum blinds, they are constructed and raised and lowered in the same way.

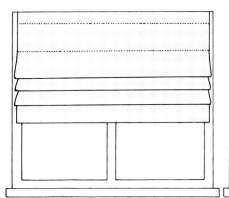 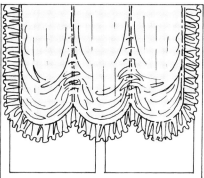 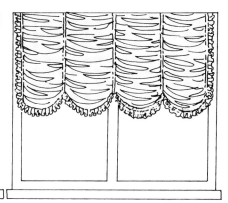

ROMAN BLINDS

Style When let down fully these fabric blinds hang flat like roller blinds; when pulled up they fold into a series of broad horizontal pleats. Plain fabrics or vertical and diagonal stripes look particularly effective.

In use Tape down each side of the blind carries a series of rings through which the cords that raise and lower the blind are threaded.

Watchpoint Lightweight fabrics, sheers or blinds wider than 1.5m need horizontal battens inserted in concealed pockets to keep the folds neat.

AUSTRIAN BLINDS

Style These blinds are raised and lowered in the same way as roman blinds but instead of folds, they gather into deep swags. When fully down they hang like a curtain. They look particularly effective made from silk, voile or moiré which allow the light to filter through; they can be made from furnishing cottons and lined for greater privacy. Add frills to the side and lower edges for a richer, decorative effect.

In use The fabric is gathered on to standard curtain heading tape; the blind can be hung from a pole, curtain track or head rail.

FESTOON BLINDS

Style Unlike austrian blinds, festoon blinds are permanently gathered into ruched swags, even when fully let down. Soft, sheer or lightweight fabrics are most suitable and the lower edge can be shaped or frilled.

In use Vertical ring-bearing tapes are sewn at 23-46cm intervals and the blind is raised in the same way as an austrian blind.

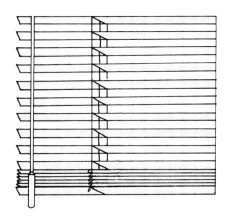 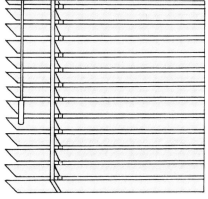 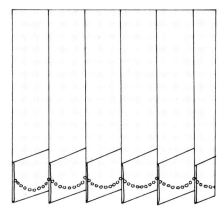

VENETIAN BLINDS

Style Most commonly made from aluminium alloy, these blinds are made to measure and come in a wide range of colours and finishes. They are also available with a mirror finish which gives a highly reflective surface, or perforated, allowing light through even when fully closed.

In use You can control the light and visibility by angling the slats using an acrylic wand or cord. The slats can be 1.5-5cm wide; the narrowest are almost invisible when the blind is lowered and fully open.

WOODEN VENETIAN BLINDS

Style Traditionally made from western red cedar, chosen for its attractive grain, lightness and stability. The wood can be left natural, stained or painted.

In use They operate in exactly the same way as metal blinds but as the 5cm slats are considerably thicker they have a deeper stack when raised.

Watchpoint These blinds work out considerably more expensive than aluminium blinds.

VERTICAL LOUVRE BLINDS

Style These stiffened strips of fabric, often with a textured weave, are made from silk; canvas, both plain or printed; or PVC, plain or perforated. The strips range from 9-13cm wide. They are attached to a track at the top and linked at the bottom, usually by a chain.

In use They can be drawn like curtains and are most often used floor to ceiling over large picture windows or patio doors. They can also be used as room dividers or to fit awkward windows.

Watchpoint Although these have been traditionally used in offices, they can be used equally successfully in the home.

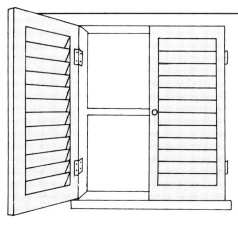 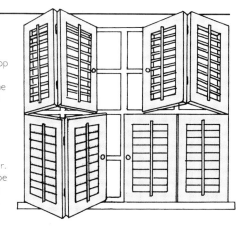

▷ PLANTATION SHUTTERS

Style Made from wood, such as pine and left natural or painted. They can be full length, or divided in half so that they can give light at the top and privacy at the bottom like a café curtain.

In use The panels are hinged to fold back and the louvres on each panel can be opened or closed independently by the central batten.

◁ LOUVRE DOOR SHUTTERS

An inexpensive treatment with a tropical flavour. Choose hinges which will allow the shutters to be opened right back against the wall. They can be solid for total light exclusion or open as normal.

MAKING CUSHIONS

Add extra comfort and a dash of colour to any room with an eye-catching collection of scatter cushions.

Cushions serve both a decorative and practical purpose in a room. Use them to soften the hard lines of modern furniture, to add colour and richness to an austere colour scheme, or as a touch of comfort and luxury.

Basic covers for square, round or rectangular cushions are quick and simple to make. They can either be left plain or you can add a decorative trim, such as piping or a frill, for a professional finish.

Choosing fabric Almost any fabric can be used – from fairly tough furnishing fabric such as heavy brocade or velvet, through cotton and canvas, to light-weight silk and lace. The limiting factor is where the cushion will be used and how much wear it will get. For cushions that will get a lot of use, choose washable fabrics.

Remnant counters are a good source of cheap cushion-sized fabric pieces and you can create a bold effect by mixing colour and pattern. For a co-ordinated look, use fabric left over from bed-covers, curtains or upholstery.

Type of opening The method of opening and its position (a side or back opening) determines the cutting measurements of the cover, so decide what you want to use before cutting out the fabric. If the cover needs regular laundering, use a zip, Velcro or press-stud opening – the cushion pad can be removed and replaced easily. A hand-sewn opening is simpler to make, but needs to be unpicked and resewn every time the pad is removed.

Always make sure that the opening is large enough to take the cushion pad easily. Ideally, the opening on a straight-edged cushion should be about 10cm shorter than the length of the side. For a round cushion, the length of the open-ing should measure about three-quarters of the diameter of the cushion.

Cushion pads The filling for a cushion must be enclosed in its own inner casing to make a pad that can be removed when the cushion cover needs washing.

Cushion pads can be bought in a range of shapes and sizes. Or you can make your own pad with a filling such as down, feathers, or shredded foam. The amount of filling needed depends on its type and the size of the cushion. A 50cm square cushion, for example, will take about 350g of down, or 900g of feathers, or about 800g of foam.

If the filling is feathers and/or down, use down-proof ticking for the casing. Otherwise calico and lining material are suitable, or you can even use the good areas of old cotton sheets. Make up the casing in the same way as a cushion cover with a hand-sewn open-ing (see overleaf).

Sewing thread The sewing thread should match the fibre content of your fabric – use polyester thread for syn-thetics, cotton thread for natural fabrics.

Cushions for comfort
A pile of soft chintz-covered cushions make this window-seat a pretty and comfortable spot. Black piping inserted at the seams pulls the mixture of plain and patterned fabrics together and links up with the smart black-trimmed Roman blinds.

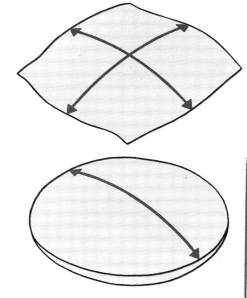

CHECK YOUR NEEDS
☐ Fabric
☐ Cushion pad
☐ Tailor's chalk
☐ Ruler
☐ Pins
☐ Long-bladed scissors
☐ Small scissors

☐ Sewing thread
☐ Needles
☐ Sewing machine

Optional extras:
☐ Piping cord and bias binding or
☐ Fabric for a frill

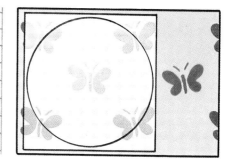

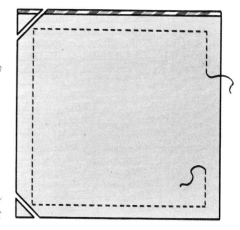

MEASURING UP △
Measure a square or rectangular pad (top) across the width and the length from seam to seam, and add a 3cm seam allowance to both measurements.

Measure a round pad (bottom) across the diameter, and add 3cm.

For a plump-looking cushion do not add a seam allowance – the cover, when sewn up, will then fit snugly.

ESTIMATING FABRIC △
If you're making several covers from the same fabric, plan your cutting layout on squared paper using a suitable scale before you buy it. Mark out an area representing the width of your fabric, then draw in cushion pieces to find the most economical arrangement, and work out the total fabric needed.

CENTRING A BOLD DESIGN △
For the best effect, position a bold design centrally on each cover section. Cut a piece of tracing paper to the size of your square, rectangle or circle and place it over the main design on the fabric as a pattern for cutting out. You may need extra fabric to get the right number of motifs.

SQUARE AND RECTANGULAR COVERS

1 *Mark out and cut fabric*
For a cover with a side opening, mark out and cut two pieces the same size – a front and a back piece. (For a back zip opening you will need two sections for the back piece – see opposite.)

Lay the fabric on a flat surface, and use a ruler and tailor's chalk to draw the cutting lines along the straight grain of the fabric. If the fabric has a pattern, make sure that it runs in the same direction for each piece.

2 *Making a hand-sewn opening* ▷
With right sides of fabric facing, tack round three sides – 1.5cm from the outer edge with a right angle at each corner. (Leave a short side of a rectangular cover untacked.) On the remaining side, tack along 5cm of the seam from each end. Stitch all tacked seams, leaving untacked section open.

At corners, cut seam allowance diagonally, close to stitching to reduce bulk. Remove tacking and neaten raw edges with zigzag stitch or over-cast by hand. Turn cover to right side and insert pad. Tack opening closed, then slipstitch. Remove tacking.

1 *Making a side zip opening* ▷
Place right sides of fabric together. On one side (short side for rectangles) tack along 5cm of the seam from each corner. Stitch, then remove tacking. Press these short seams flat, and press seam allowance of opening to wrong side.

Lay zip (of the same size as the opening) face up. Place open section of seam (with wrong side of fabric to zip) directly over the zip teeth, and tack zip in place. On right side of fabric, stitch down both sides of zip and across the short ends as close to the teeth as possible. Remove tacking.

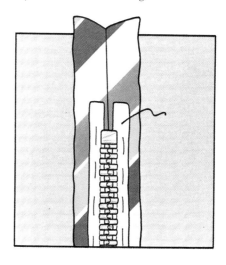

2 *Stitch remaining sides*
With right sides of fabric facing and the zip open, tack and stitch round the other three sides. Remove tacking, clip corners, and neaten raw edges with zigzag stitch or overcast by hand. Turn right side out, and insert pad.

ROUND CUSHION COVERS

The success of a round cover depends on cutting a perfect circle from the fabric, so make a paper pattern first.

For a plump cushion, omit seam allowances from the paper pattern.

Zips are best inserted across the back of round cushions; zips in the side seams may cause puckering.

1 *Draw a paper pattern ▷*
Cut a square of paper slightly larger than the cushion pad and fold it into quarters. Tie string round a pencil and cut this off to half the diameter of the cushion plus 1.5cm for seam allowance.

Lay the folded paper on a board and pin the end of the string to the point of the folded corner. With string taut and pencil held upright, draw a quarter circle on the paper.

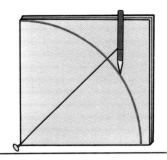

2 *Cut out ▷*
Carefully cut along the pencil line through all four layers of paper. Open out the paper and use as a pattern for cutting out two circles of fabric for a cover. (If you want a zip in the back, you will need a different pattern for the back piece – see below.)

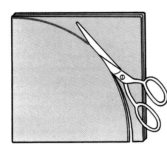

3 *Making a hand-sewn opening ▽*
With right sides of fabric facing, tack round the circumference with a 1.5cm seam allowance, leaving an opening sufficient to take the cushion pad. Stitch.

Remove tacking, and cut notches into the seam allowance at regular intervals. Turn cover to right side and insert pad. Tack the opening closed. Slipstitch. Remove tacking.

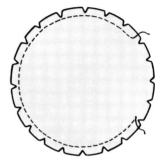

1 *Making a side zip opening ▷*
With right sides facing, pin fabric circles together, leaving an opening the length of the zip. Tack seam for 2.5cm either side of the opening, with a 1.5cm allowance. Stitch. Remove tacking, and press short seams flat.

Pin and tack zip into opening, easing fabric slightly to allow for the curve. Stitch. Open zip and place fabric circles together, right sides facing. Tack together, then stitch. Remove tacking, and notch seam allowance (see diagram above). Turn cover right side out and insert pad.

1 *Making a back zip opening*
First use a circular paper pattern to cut one piece of fabric for the front. Then, using a zip length about 10cm shorter than the diameter, mark a straight line across the paper pattern where the zip is to be fitted – either centred or off centre. Cut the paper pattern along this line.

2 *Cut two back pieces ▷*
Place the back patterns on the fabric, adding an extra 1.5cm seam allowance to both straight edges where the zip is to be inserted. Cut out the two sections for the back of the cushion cover.

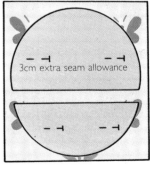

3cm extra seam allowance

3 *Insert the zip ▷*
With right sides of the two back pieces facing and raw edges matching, tack and stitch up to 5cm from both ends of the straight edge. Remove tacking and sew in zip (as for square cover).

Tack together front and back of cover (with right sides facing and zip open). Stitch all round. Remove tacking and notch around the circumference. Turn cover right side out and insert pad.

OTHER OPENING METHODS

In place of a zip you can use a length of press stud tape or Velcro. Make up the cover – for a square or round cushion pad – in the same way as for a hand-sewn side opening. Place tape or Velcro on either side of the opening and slipstitch or machine in place.

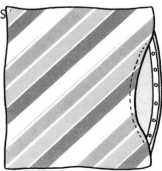

PROFESSIONAL TOUCHES

Cushion covers can be trimmed in a number of ways. For a smart look, add a neat trim to seams using piping cord covered with fabric. Or use a gathered frill, in matching or contrasting fabric, to give a soft and pretty finish.

Both these trimmings are sandwiched between the two cushion pieces and stitched in place with the main cushion cover seams.

PIPING

Piping cord comes in several thicknesses – a thicker cord will stand out more from the seam. It should be used in a continuous strip so add an extra 5cm to the length of cord required for joining up (see below).

Cover with fabric cut on the bias grain, wide enough to enclose the cord plus 2cm for seam allowance. Ready-made bias binding is convenient and comes in several widths and colours.

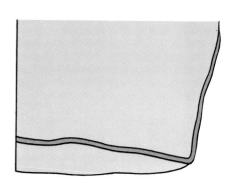

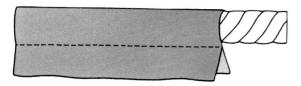

1 *Cover the piping cord △*
Place the cord along the centre of the wrong side of an opened up strip of purchased bias binding. Then fold the bias binding in half over the cord and tack in place. Using a zipper foot, stitch as close to the cord as possible. Remove tacking.

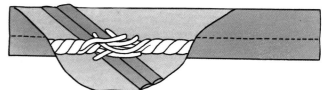

2 *Join lengths of piping cord △*
Join lengths of bias binding using a 5mm flat seam stitched at an angle along the grain of the tape. Then overlap two ends of cord. To make a smooth join, unravel the strands at each end by 2.5cm, and trim each strand to a slightly different length before intertwining them.

3 *Add piping to cushion cover seam ▷*
For best results, use piping on cushions with a back zip opening. Insert zip as described on page 68. With tailor's chalk, mark a 1.5cm seam allowance on right side of either front or back of cushion cover. Position piping along this marked line, with raw edges of piping cord fabric matching raw edges of cushion cover. Tack in place, curving it slightly round corners to avoid sharp angles. Clip seam allowance at corners to reduce bulk.

With right sides facing and zip open, tack front and back of cushion cover together with piping sandwiched in the middle. Using a zipper foot, stitch all round as close to piping as possible. Remove tacking.

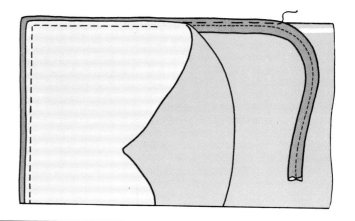

A GATHERED FRILL

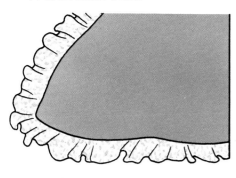

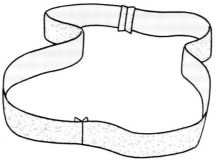

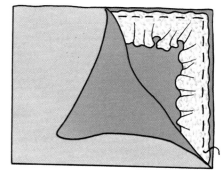

1 *Measure up and cut out*
A narrow frill is most easily made from a double thickness of fabric. Decide the finished width of the frill, add a 1.5cm seam allowance and double this measurement.

To calculate length of frill needed, measure the distance around the outside of your cushion pad. Add a 1.5cm seam allowance (plus 1.5cm for each join necessary to make up the length), and double this measurement.

2 *Prepare the frill △*
With right sides facing, join short ends of fabric with 1.5cm seams to make a continuous frill. Fold fabric in half lengthways, wrong sides facing, and press.

Work two rows of gathering stitches through the layers – 1.5cm and 1cm from the raw edge. For even gathers, work along half the frill length, then cut the threads. Use a new thread for gathering the remaining length.

3 *Add frill to cushion cover △*
Fold one of the cushion cover pieces in half, and mark each end of the fold with tailor's chalk. Open flat again.

Pin frill to the right side of one cushion cover piece, with raw edges matching and each break in the gathering threads on one of the chalk marks. Pull the gathering threads evenly to fit the frill to the edge. Tack and stitch. Then complete as for square or round cushion cover.

SIMPLE GUSSETED CUSHIONS

Make a firm, tailored cushion by adding a generous side gusset to the cover.

This type of cushion has a top and a bottom piece, joined by a strip of fabric called a gusset. The result is a deep, firm cushion with a neat tailored shape.

Gusseted cushions can be square, rectangular or round for use on a plain hard chair, bench or window seat; they're also useful for extra floor seating and make excellent footstools.

Long, firm bolsters are really round cushions with an elongated gusset. Traditionally used at ends of sofas, bolsters make good backrests – particularly when placed along the back of a divan, for example, to support a row of scatter cushions or pillows.

Covers can be left plain or you can emphasize the shape of the cushion with strong piped seams or a decorative gusset: pick out one of the colours in a patterned fabric, or use a toning or contrasting colour to add emphasis to a plain cover. If you want to make a decorative panel insert, make the panelled piece before making up the cover.

Cushion pads A pad or block of solid foam is the best choice for cushions with a gusset as it retains its shape and looks neat. Foam, however, tends to crumble with regular use so you will need an inner cover for the pad. This should be made out of a strong fabric such as pre-shrunk calico, lining material or even old cotton sheets.

Buy foam at least 4cm thick for scatter cushions, deeper for more substantial seating.

Choosing fabric Cushions usually get a lot of wear so choose strong, washable fabrics: furnishing fabrics – such as velvet, corduroy, linen or heavy cotton – are ideal. If the fabric is not pre-shrunk, wash it first to reduce shrinkage.

To work out how much fabric you need for a gusseted cushion, see overleaf. If seams are to be piped, you'll need extra fabric for cutting bias strips or you can use ready-made bias binding.

Types of opening A zip inserted in one side of the cover makes it easy to remove the cushion pad for laundering.

For a square or rectangular cover, the zip should be long enough to extend around each of the two adjoining corners by at least 5cm – this makes it easier to insert and remove the cushion pad. For a round or bolster cover, the zip should measure at least half the circumference of the pad.

If you don't want a zipped opening (or you're making an inner cover), omit instructions given for inserting a zip. Attach the gusset to one cover piece. Then attach the other cover piece: stitch along three sides, and about 5cm in from each corner on the fourth side, leaving a central opening. Insert the cushion pad and neatly slipstitch the opening closed.

Before you begin making up gusseted cushion covers, see the previous chapter for instructions on making basic covers and cushion pads.

Comfortable assets
Cushions with a gusset are ideal for adding comfort to a hard wooden chair, bench or window seat. Here, an attractive piped trim is added to the seams for a more tailored finish on these shaped cushions.

SQUARE AND RECTANGULAR GUSSETED COVERS

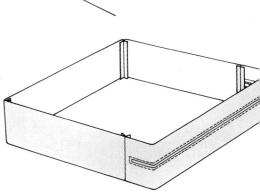

length · width · depth · zip position

CHECK YOUR NEEDS
- ☐ Fabric
- ☐ Cushion pad
- ☐ Zip
- ☐ Tailor's chalk
- ☐ Ruler
- ☐ Pins
- ☐ Long-bladed scissors for cutting fabric
- ☐ Short-bladed scissors for trimming
- ☐ Sewing machine
- ☐ Sewing thread
- ☐ Needles

For round covers and bolsters:
- ☐ Paper
- ☐ String
- ☐ Pencil
- ☐ Drawing pin
- ☐ Cutting board

Optional:
- ☐ Piping cord
- ☐ Bias binding or fabric strips

2 *Measure the gusset* ◁
The gusset is made up of four pieces: one front, two sides, and one back piece which takes the zip.
For the back gusset piece, cut a rectangle measuring the length of the zip plus 3cm seam allowance, by the depth of the pad plus 6cm seam allowance (to allow for zip opening).
For the front and side gussets, measure the length and depth of the remaining cushion sides, allowing 3cm all round for seam allowances. Cut out gusset pieces.

1 *Measure top and base* △
For the top and bottom of the cover, measure the width and length of the top of the pad, and add 3cm to both measurements for seam allowance. Then cut out.

3 *Insert zip* ▷
Cut the back gusset piece in half along its length. Turn a 1.5cm seam allowance to the wrong side along one edge of each half and press.
Lay back gussets side by side on the table (wrong sides up) with folded sides together and place zip centrally, face down. Pin, tack and stitch the zip in position.

4 *Make up the gusset* ▷
With right sides facing and taking a 1.5cm seam allowance, pin the ends of the gusset side sections to the front and back sections to form a square or rectangle which fits snugly round the cushion pad.
Tack and stitch. Secure ends of stitching firmly, remove tacking and press seams open.

5 *Sew to main fabric* ▷
With right sides facing and corners matching, pin and tack the gusset to one main piece of cushion cover, then stitch in place with a 1.5cm seam. If you want a piped trim, make up the piping (as shown on page 70) and insert in the seams between gusset and main pieces at this stage – see opposite.
Open the zip, and attach the remaining cover piece in the same way. Press all the seams towards the gusset. Turn the cover through to right side, press and insert cushion pad.

Corner seams
To ensure a neat square finish at corners, stitch up to the corner, then insert the machine needle right into the fabric at this point. Lift the presser foot and pivot the fabric round the needle, turning it to the correct position for stitching down the other side. Replace presser foot and continue stitching.
Finish each corner by clipping into seam allowance, up to the stitching; then snip diagonally across the seam allowance, close to stitching, to eliminate bulk.

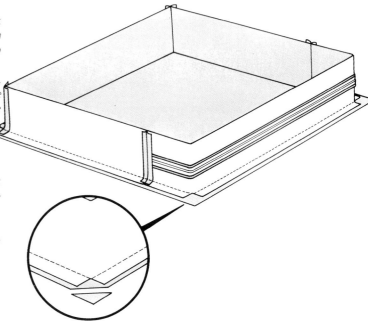

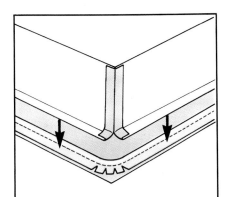

PIPED GUSSETED COVERS

Make up two strips of piping, each the same length as the finished gusset plus an overlap of 2.5cm. With raw edges together, attach piping to both main pieces of cover. Clip into piping seam allowance at corners, then complete the cover.

ROUND GUSSETED COVERS

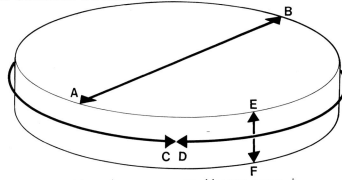

1 *Measure top and base* △
For the top and bottom of the cover, measure across the diameter of the cushion pad (A-B) and add 3cm seam allowance.

Make a paper pattern to this size (as for a basic round cushion cover, steps 1-2, page 69) and cut out two circles of fabric.

2 *Measure gusset* △
For the gusset, measure the circumference (C-D) and depth (E-F) of the cushion pad. Cut one rectangle measuring half the circumference plus 3cm, by the depth plus 3cm.

For the zipped half of the gusset, cut a second rectangle measuring half the circumference plus 3cm, by the depth plus 6cm (to allow for the zip opening).

3 *Insert zip*
Cut the gusset for the zip in half along its length. Turn under 1.5cm seam allowance along the cut edge of both halves and press.

Lay two halves on the table (wrong sides up) with folded sides together and place zip centrally, face down. Pin and tack in place, and stitch close to the teeth all round.

4 *Make up the gusset* ▷
With right sides facing and taking a 1.5cm seam, pin the short ends of the two gusset pieces together to form a circle to go round the cushion.

Tack and stitch, leaving 1.5cm unstitched at each end of seams. Secure ends of stitching firmly, then press seams open.

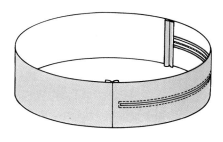

BRIGHT IDEA

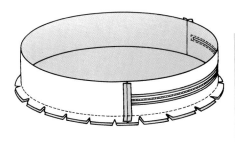

5 *Sew to main fabric* △
With the zip open and right sides facing, pin, tack and stitch the gusset to one cover piece and then the other.

Remove tacking and notch seam allowances at 2.5cm intervals all round to ease the fabric and give a neat appearance to the seam on the right side. Press seams towards gusset. Turn cover right side out, and insert pad.

Piping
If you want a piped trim, make up piping (as shown on page 70) and attach to each circular cover piece. Then attach gusset, but notch the gusset seam allowances before stitching together.

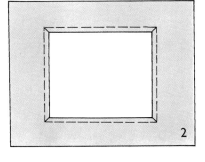

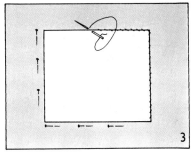

DECORATIVE PANEL INSERTS

For a pretty patchwork effect, add a panel of contrasting fabric to a cushion cover. Use fabric offcuts, embroidery or lace: for strength, back lace first with a piece of fabric such as silk, satin or tiny cotton print.

Set the panel into the cover piece before making up the cushion cover.

1 Decide the finished size of the panel to be inserted in the cover, then add a 1.5cm seam allowance all round and cut from fabric.

2 Using tailor's chalk, mark out the finished panel on the front of the cover. Then draw another line

1.5cm inside the first for a seam allowance, and cut out a hole along this inner line. Clip into the corners of seam allowance and press seam to wrong side (if the cut-out is round, clip at regular intervals all round the circle).

3 With right sides facing up, pin the panel in position under the hole in the cover. Tack, then slipstitch or topstitch, or use zigzag stitch for a decorative edge.

MAKING BOLSTER CUSHIONS

A bolster is basically a variation of a round gusseted cushion, with the gusset depth extended to the length of the bolster and sewn into a long tube of fabric. This type of cushion is particularly useful on beds and divans.

Zips The zip for a bolster cover is inserted in the side seam of the tube and should measure at least half the circumference of the bolster so that the pad can be put in easily.

1 *Measure and cut* ▷
For the main piece, measure the length (A-B) and the circumference (C-D) of the bolster pad. Add a 3cm seam allowance to both measurements and cut a piece of fabric to these dimensions.

For the end pieces, measure the diameter of the pad (E-F) and add 3cm. Make a paper pattern as for a round cover and cut two circles of fabric.

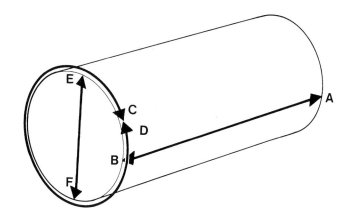

2 *Stitch main piece* ▷
Fold the main piece of fabric in half, with the two edges that are the length of the bolster together and right sides facing.

Pin, tack and stitch along seam allowance from each end, leaving a central opening the length of the zip. Remove tacking; press seam flat, and press seam allowance of opening to wrong side. Pin, tack and stitch zip into opening.

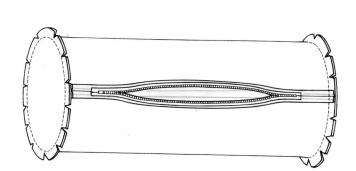

3 *Stitch the ends* ▷
Open the zip. With right sides facing, pin, tack and stitch the two end circles to the main cover piece.

If you want a piped trim, stitch the piping round the ends of the main cover piece before attaching the ends.

Notch round the seam allowances at 2.5cm intervals. Press seams towards the end circles of fabric. Turn cover right side out, press and insert cushion pad.

Versatile seating
Fat, padded bolster cushions help to turn this fold-away bed into a comfortable daytime sofa.

CLEVER WAYS WITH CUSHION TRIMS

Cushions add a touch of comfort to any room. Give them added style with one or more of these edging ideas.

A welcoming pile of cushions is a stylish addition to a living room or bedroom. For extra effect, you can give the cushions an individual trim, choosing the finish to suit the atmosphere of the room. For example, frills, lace and ribbon trims add a romantic touch to a bedroom; piping, pleats and a flat trim look smart in a more formal setting.

The variety of styles and shapes for cushions is almost infinite – the effects you achieve will depend on the mixture of fabrics you use as well as the combination of piping, trimming and binding. It is an area where you can really invent your own finishes. They are small and relatively inexpensive to make, and there is no reason why you shouldn't use oddments of fabric.

Contrast piping and double frills are obvious ways of combining different fabrics and colours in one item, but there are several other ways of creating a co-ordinated effect. You can appliqué shapes on to the front of the cushions, or edge a flat cushion trim with zigzag stitch in a contrasting colour. Ribbon bows, or lengths of ribbon top-stitched in place give further scope for decorative finishes.

As well as mixing fabrics, try mixing different shapes when making cushions: square, round, rectangular and even heart-shaped cushions look effective piled at the head of a bed. Once you have learned some of the tricks of the trade, you can go on to design your own shapes – for example, what about a cat-shaped cushion, or a cushion designed to look like a huge sunflower?

Sewing techniques As well as giving you ideas for specific shapes and trims, this chapter deals with some sewing techniques which can be applied in other situations. For example, we show you how to notch the seam allowance on curved seams to get a flat finish, and how to trim away the bulk c fabric from seams (where there is piping and a frill) to achieve a smooth finish.

Always remember when sewing that you should press your work at each stage. This not only keeps the fabric crisp and easy to work, but helps to produce a better finish. Pressing a seam after stitching it, for example, helps to knit the seam together. Don't be tempted to leave pressing until the work is finished – you may not be able to get at all the corners and angles.

CHOOSE YOUR FABRICS

For hard-wearing cushions which will keep their good looks, choose furnishing cottons and linen unions. Slub weaves and raw silks can look particularly effective in a traditional setting. For a more glamorous touch, look at satins and fine silks. You can use dressmaking fabrics if the cushions will not get a lot of wear – but be careful to keep them away from direct sunlight, as dressmaking fabrics fade faster than furnishing fabrics.

Where possible, use remnants of fabric from other furnishings in the room (curtains, bedlinen, tablecloths), so that you achieve a co-ordinated look for a minimum outlay.

If you are adding piping, make your own bias binding where possible, as ready-made binding is usually made from poor-quality cotton.

MEASURING UP

If you have ready-made cushion pads, measure them to find the finished measurement required for the cover. Add 1.5cm seam allowances all round for the front panel of the cushion. Allow an extra 3cm in one direction for inserting a zip in the back panel of the cushion.

If you are making your own cushion pads, you may find it more economical to make the pads to suit the width of the fabric, or the size of the remnants, you are using for the cover. For example, if you are making cushion pads from ticking fabric 90cm wide, by making the cushions 27cm square you will be able to get three cushions from 60cm of fabric, whereas if the cushions

All puffed up
Piles of cushions, with frills and ruching, add importance to the head of a bed. The heart-shaped cushion and ruching have been made up in a lettuce green fabric, giving an overall green look to a fabric which is primarily cream, blue and apricot.

are 30cm square you will need 1m of fabric for the same number of pads.

Frills To calculate the length of a frill, measure the perimeter of the cushion, multiply by 1½ and add 1.5cm for seam allowances where necessary. The width of the frill will depend on the effect you want. The larger the cushion, the wider the frill you will need to achieve a balanced look.

Seam allowances will depend on the finish you choose: a double-thickness frill (where the fabric is folded in half down its length) requires a seam allowance down each long edge of 1.5cm. A bound edge requires a single 1.5cm seam allowance, and a hemmed edge requires 1.5cm down one long edge and a 1cm allowance down the other edge for a 5mm wide double hem.

Pleats For a pleated finish, you will need a strip of fabric three times the length of the perimeter of the cushion (plus 1.5cm seam allowances where necess-ary). The width is calculated in the same way as the width of the frill.

Binding Binding for piping should be cut on the bias, 35mm wide. Binding for trims can be cut to any width, and in most cases (since it does not have to be eased round corners) it can be cut on the straight, which makes cutting easier. Whichever way it is cut, allow a 1cm turning allowance down each long edge, and 1.5cm for joining lengths together where necessary.

CHECK YOUR NEEDS
- [ ] Selection of fabrics
- [ ] Cushion pad
- [ ] Needles and pins
- [ ] Sewing thread
- [ ] Sewing machine
- [ ] Scissors

- [ ] Tape measure

According to your design:
- [ ] Piping cord
- [ ] Bias binding
- [ ] Ruler
- [ ] Dressmaker's chalk

CLOSURES FOR CUSHIONS
The various ways of closing the cushion are described earlier in Making Cushions (pages 68-69). In this chapter, we assume that you will set the zip into the back of the cushion – which gives the neatest effect. You will have to adapt the instructions if you choose another form of closure.

CLIPPING AND NOTCHING
These techniques are used on curved seams, to enable the seam to lie flat. Notching is used on external (convex) seams and clipping on internal curves. Thus, on a circular cushion, you have to notch the seam allowance to reduce the bulk once the cover is finished.

1 *Notching convex seams* ▷
Notching involves clipping V-shapes out of the seam allowance of external corners or curves, cutting in as close to the seam as possible without cutting the stitches. The sharper the curve, the more notches you will need. Trimming away the seam allowance will also reduce the bulk, which can look ugly once the cover is finished.

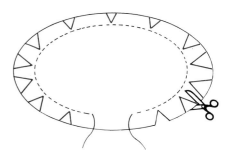

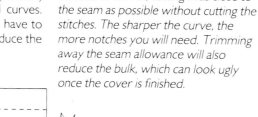

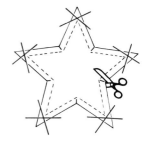

2 *Clipping corners* △
Clipping across corners has the same effect as cutting notches: the bulk of the seam allowance is removed. Corners which are sharper than 90° should have even more of the seam allowance clipped away (see step 3).

3 *Clipping concave curves* △
If you are making a shaped cushion, you may have sharp internal angles or curved seams. The solution is to clip into the seam allowance, clipping as close to the stitching line as you can. Once turned out, the seam allowance

will be able to stretch so that the shape is not distorted. On a sharp internal angle, a single clip should be sufficient. On gently curved seams, a series of clips will be needed. The sharper the curve, the closer together they should be made.

GATHERS
You need to gather fabric when making a frill, or adding a ruched insert. It is also a useful technique for easing the fullness at corners when making soft square or rectangular cushions with puffy, round-ed corners. For a double frill, fold in half along length first.

1 *Gathering stitches* ▽
Cut the strip to be gathered 1½ times the length of the seam where it is to be inserted. Fold the ungathered frill into four even sections and mark the fold lines. To gather strips of fabric, make two parallel rows of running stitch, a couple of millimetres apart,

within the seam allowance, close to the seam line. It is best to knot the thread at the end, so that you can draw up the gathers from both ends if necessary. Make each stitch about 5mm long. Line up the rows of stitches for crisp gathers, but for a more delicate effect, stagger the stitches.

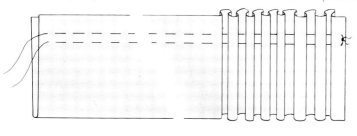

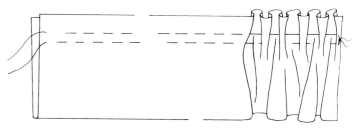

2 Drawing up fullness ▷

Once you have made the lines of stitches, draw up the fullness until the length of the frill matches the perimeter of the cushion. This is often easier if the gathering is done in sections. Put a pin in the frill at the end of the row of gathering stitches, and wind the ends of the gathering stitches round it to anchor it. Then move the gathers along the gathering thread until they are evenly distributed. Divide the perimeter of the panel the frill is to be stitched to into four equal sections and mark the edge. Then start pinning the frill to the front panel of the cushion so that the gathers are held in place, and the marks on the frill match the marks on the edge of the panel.

If the frill is to go round a rectangular cushion, you will need to group the gathers together and arrange them so there is extra fullness at the corners.

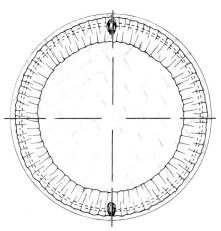

3 Tack in place

Once you are happy with the effect of the gathers, tack the frill in place.

It is worth taking quite small, neat stitches so that the gathers cannot be pushed out of place by the foot of the sewing machine when you come to stitch it.

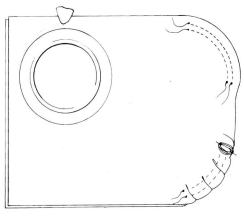

4 Soft square corners △

To make a soft, square cushion and avoid spiky corners, mark a curved stitching line at each corner, drawing round a plate, or similar curved shape. Trim away the seam allowance 1.5cm from the marked line. Gather the corners by hand and tack gathers in place. Insert piping into seam to hold gathers firmly and give a neat finish.

RUCHING

This is a variation of gathering, where both edges of the gathered section are stitched (rather than just one edge, as on a frill). You can insert a ruched section into any shaped cushion. Here we give instructions for a circular cushion with ruching round the edge. The measurements given are for a 40cm diameter circular cushion with a 20cm diameter centre surrounded by a 20cm wide ruched panel.

1 Cut out fabrics

Cut out fabric for the back panel as usual, cutting two sections which can have a zip inserted between them to form a 43cm diameter panel. For the front panel, cut a circle 23cm in diameter and a panel 192cm by 23cm for the ruched section (the length of the section to be ruched is 1½ times the circumference of the finished cover, plus seam allowance). Cut out binding for piping if necessary (both edges of the ruched area may be piped if wished).

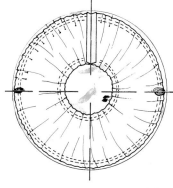

2 Gather panel to be ruched △

Join short ends with a flat seam. Mark the panel and the edge of the two circular sections into four equal parts. Make two lines of gathering stitches down each side of the panel to be ruched. Make the stitches even for a more formal effect, or stagger them for a more random effect. Draw up one side to fit round the central circle of fabric, matching marked points and distributing fullness evenly. Pin, tack and stitch in place. Trim (or layer – see below) seam allowance and press towards ruched area.

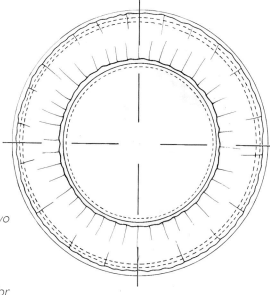

3 Finish outer seam △

Draw up the outer gathered edge to match the back panel of the cushion cover. Pin, tack and stitch in place. Notch and trim seam allowances and press before turning right side out and inserting cushion pad.

LAYERING

This technique involves trimming away seam allowances (of cushion cover panels, piping and/or frills) in such a way as to prevent a sharp step showing when the cushion cover is turned right-side out. It is particularly useful when working with bulky fabrics.

1 Stitch seams

Cut out fabrics and stitch seams in the usual way, taking 1.5cm seam allowances. Press.

2 Trim seam allowances ▷

Trim each seam allowance in turn, trimming more from the piping and/or frill than from the main fabric, so that the seam allowances are all different widths. The narrowest should be about 3mm wide, and each subsequent seam allowance you trim should be 2-3mm longer than the previous one. Press to one side and neaten seam allowances together (with zigzag stitch) before turning right side out and inserting cushion pad.

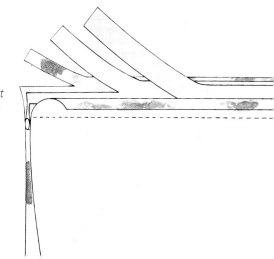

PLEATED FRILLS

A crisply-pleated frill is a smart trim for a rectangular cushion. For a generous finish, allow three times the perimeter of the cushion when making up the trim. Once the pleats are prepared, insert them into the seam as for a frill. Include 1.5cm seam allowances. Where possible, arrange seams so they fall inside the pleats.

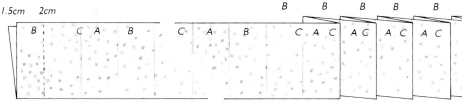

1 Knife pleats △
Use a double width of fabric, folded in half down its length, or neaten the edge. Decide on a suitable width for

each pleat (2-3cm usually looks good). Leave 1.5cm for seam allowance, then mark the pleating lines. Pleat the strip, so that point A meets point C.

2 Box pleats ▷
For box pleats, prepare the strip and mark it. Follow the diagram to pleat it, folding one point A up to point C and the next back to the same point.

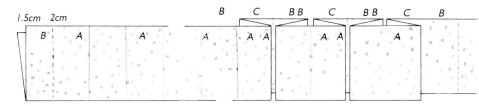

QUICK COVER WITH FLAT TRIM

This cover is easy to make if your sewing machine does satin stitch.

1 Cut out fabric
For the front panel, cut fabric 7cm larger all round than the cushion pad. For the back panel, cut fabric 7cm larger all round, plus 3cm in one direction to allow for zip. Set in zip.

BRIGHT IDEA

Pillowcase-style closure To save the expense of a zip, and the nuisance of hand-sewn openings, make a tuck-in similar to a pillowcase. Cut the front panel as usual. For the back panel, cut two pieces of fabric, one the size of the back plus 1.5cm seam allowance all round. Cut the second panel the same width as the first by 10cm deep. Neaten one edge of the first back panel and one long edge of the second, taking 1cm double hems. Lay the smaller panel on the larger panel, right side of the smaller facing the wrong side of the larger. Tack together, and make up the cushion as though they were a single panel.

▷ Set and match
By using fabrics from the same range it is easy to achieve an instantly co-ordinated effect over a wide range of shapes and styles.

2 Stitch seam ▷
Lay the front panel on back panel, wrong sides facing and raw edges matching. Pin and tack panels together, 7cm inside raw edges. Topstitch the panels together, making two rows of stitching for decorative effect.

3 Neaten edges ▷
Tack outer edges of flat trim together, 1cm from raw edge. Use a fine satin stitch to join layers of border, then trim away raw edges, cutting as close to the line of satin stitch as you can.

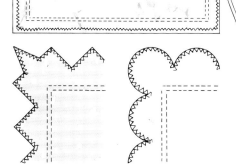

4 Shaped edges ▷
For a more striking effect, after tacking the layers of the trim together, mark scallops or a deep zigzag on the trim with dressmaker's chalk. Stitch with satin stitch as before, following the marked line. Carefully trim away the raw edges.

A SIMPLE SLIP-ON LAMPSHADE

Start lampshade making with this simple slip-on shade which is easy to remove for cleaning.

A slip-on lampshade is the simplest of all shades to make – there is no complicated fitting, no special shaping, and no taping and sewing to the frame. The shade is attached to the frame by a ribboned casing at the top, and held in place with an elasticated casing at the bottom so you can easily slip it off the frame for cleaning. **Choose a frame** with a round or oval top and bottom ring. The top ring should be smaller than the bottom ring and the struts must be straight as in an empire or drum, or bowed out as in a tiffany. Do not use frames with a shaped bottom edge.

A shade with a narrow top and a wide bottom throws a pool of light downwards and is ideal for hanging over a dining table, particularly if it is on a rise-and-fall fitting.

Preparing the frame Lampshade frames are available in plain metal or coated with white plastic.

Plain metal frames must be painted, or they will rust and mark the shade. Before painting, remove any rust by rubbing down with sandpaper and file off any rough or sharp spots. Paint the struts and rings with white enamel paint, but do not paint the gimbal (the centre ring that attaches to the light bulb holder).

Choosing lampshade fabric The thinner and lighter coloured the fabric, the more light will shine through the shade. A thick, dark fabric will only throw the light from the top and bottom of the shade.

Is lining necessary? A lining makes a shade look neater and more professional inside, and also helps to reflect light from inside the shade – a pale colour is the best choice, particularly for a dark fabric shade. A lining will also help to prevent the light bulb from showing through a very thin, light fabric.

Lining does, of course, add extra bulk to the shade fabric. If the top ring of the frame is much smaller than the bottom, as with a large tiffany, this could make it impossible to gather up the fabric tightly enough to fit. In this case, use a lightweight lining such as lawn.

A pool of light
Make up the lampshade in a fabric which matches the soft furnishings in a room. If the fabric is liable to shrink, pre-wash both it and the lining before making up the shade.

CHECK YOUR NEEDS
- ☐ Lampshade frame
- ☐ Fabric for shade
- ☐ Lining fabric (optional)
- ☐ 4mm ribbon for top casing
- ☐ 4mm elastic for bottom casing
- ☐ Frill or beading for bottom edge (optional)

plus:
- ☐ Safety pin
- ☐ Scissors
- ☐ Pins
- ☐ Needles
- ☐ Sewing thread

CALCULATING THE AMOUNT OF FABRIC

To calculate the length of fabric needed, measure the frame height, following the curve or slope of the side (A).

Add 5.5cm at the top for the casing (B) – this will form a gathered frill that stands above the ring and hides it.

Then add an allowance for the elasticated casing at the bottom (C). The depth of the bottom casing should not be more than one fifth of the height of the frame, so that heat from the bulb can escape. For example, for a 30cm high frame, you need a 6cm casing. To calculate the casing allowance, double the size of the finished casing and add 5mm.

To calculate the width of fabric needed, measure the circumference (round the outside) of the shade at its largest point and add 2cm for seam allowance.

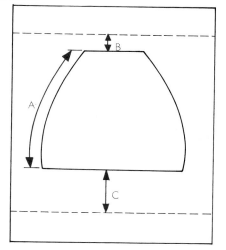

1 *Cut out fabric*
Cut out a piece of fabric to the dimensions required. Cut an identical piece in lining fabric if applicable.

If the circumference of the shade is greater than the width of your fabric, you will need to join two pieces of fabric. Measure half the circumference of the frame and add 2cm for seam allowances, then cut two pieces of fabric to these measurements.

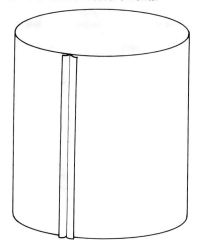

2 *Join main fabric △*
With right sides facing, join the fabric for the shade with 1cm seams to make a tube. Repeat for the lining fabric.

For unlined shades, neaten the seam edges with a machine zigzag stitch or oversew by hand, then press. Do not neaten seam edges if you are lining the lampshade fabric (see Step 3).

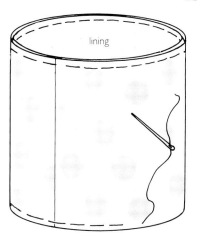

3 *Attach lining △*
Press fabric and lining seams open, then place wrong sides together and tack round top and bottom edges. From now on, treat the fabric and lining as one.

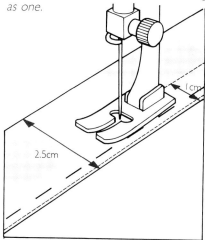

4 *Make top casing △*
Turn 5mm to wrong side along top edge of fabric and tack. Turn a further 2.5cm to wrong side and tack.

Then sew along lower edge of turn and again 1cm higher up to make a casing for the ribbon. Remove tacking.

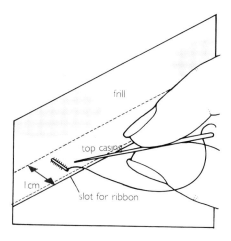

5 *Cut a slit in top casing △*
With a small pair of pointed scissors, cut a slit on the inside of the top casing through only one layer of fabric (and lining if applicable) just large enough to thread the ribbon through. Overcast edges of slit to neaten.

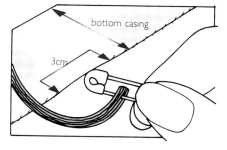

6 *Make the bottom casing △*
Turn 5mm to wrong side along bottom edge of shade and tack. Then turn the fabric again to the wrong side to the depth of the bottom casing (which you have already calculated) and tack. Slipstitch along the edge of this casing, leaving 3cm open.

Attach a small safety pin to one end of elastic and thread it through the casing. Pin the ends of elastic together to stop them slipping back.

7 *Insert ribbon in top casing*
Measure the top ring circumference, add 20cm, and cut a length of 4mm ribbon to this length. Then thread the ribbon through the top casing in the same way as elastic (see Step 6); pin the ends of ribbon together to secure.

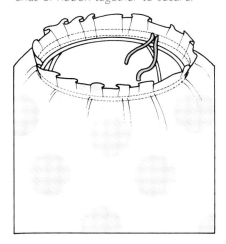

8 *Fit the shade △*
Gently pull the tube of fabric over the frame, aligning at least one seam with a metal strut and the top casing with the top ring of the frame.

Draw up the ribbon in the top casing until the shade fits the ring. Make necessary adjustments so that gathers are even and a small frill stands above them. Knot the two ends of ribbon around the ring to hold the shade.

9 *Adjust the bottom casing*
Unpin the elastic in the bottom casing and pull it up underneath the frame until the fabric is taut. Pin and sew the elastic together securely; cut off any surplus and close the gap in the casing with slipstitch.

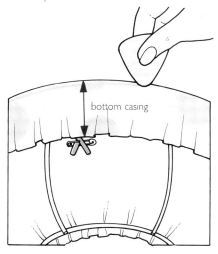

bottom casing

10 *Adding a trim △*
If you are adding a trim (see overleaf), pin the elastic but do not cut off surplus. Mark round the bottom of the frame with a line of tailor's chalk. Untie the ribbon, remove shade from frame and stitch trim in position on marked line.

BRIGHT IDEA

A READY-MADE FINISH

For a shade with a ready-made trim along the bottom edge use broderie anglaise, or a similar fabric, with one pre-shaped edge.

This type of shade is only suitable for a frame that has a bottom that is wider than the top – a tiffany shade or tapered drum, for example. Cut the fabric to the height of the frame, plus top casing allowance, plus the depth of the drop you want to hang below the bottom edge of the frame. For the width, measure the circumference of the bottom edge of the frame and add 2cm for a seam allowance. If you are adding a lining

for a fine fabric like broderie anglaise, the depth of the lining should omit the bottom drop allowance: simply add a 5mm turning instead.

Follow the basic instructions for making up and fitting a slip-on shade but do not make a casing at the bottom. Slip the fabric over the frame and pull up the ribbon at the top. The shade will overhang the bottom of the frame, giving a shaped bottom edge.

If the broderie anglaise has slots for threading a ribbon, as shown in the picture, you can use them to hold the shade firmly to the frame.

FINISHES FOR THE BOTTOM EDGE

Although the bottom of the shade can be left plain, a sewn-on trim can look very attractive. A fringe of colourful beads or a frill made from a co-ordinating fabric or lace can add an extra soft and pretty touch.

Adding a patterned beaded fringe ▷

To calculate roughly how many beads you will need, use coloured pencils to mark out a pattern repeat on graph paper. Then count up how many beads of each colour you will need for one pattern repeat and multiply by the number of repeats needed to trim the shade. Add a drop bead for each beaded strand.

Start each strand with a drop bead slotted on a single thread. Then make a double thread by passing the loose end back through the eye of the needle and slot the remaining beads on to it according to the pattern. Neatly sew ends of threads to chalk-marked fold of shade.

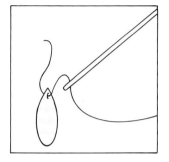 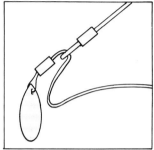

Adding a frill ▷

To calculate fabric for a frill, measure the circumference of the bottom of the frame and cut a piece of fabric or lace 1½ times this length. Neaten both long raw edges of frill with a double hem and join short ends to make a complete circle.

Gather the frill up evenly to fit the bottom of the frame. Remove the elastic in the bottom casing of the shade and stretch the fabric out. Then topstitch the frill to the shade along the chalk-marked line, taking care not to sew over the 3cm gap left in the casing.

Rethread the elastic and secure, replace fabric on frame, knot top ribbon in place and pull bottom casing elastic up to fit. Sew elastic together, cut off surplus and slipstitch the gap in the casing closed.

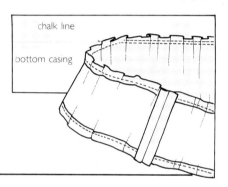

Adding a scalloped edge

For a neat scalloped edge which fits round the frame exactly, first make a pattern by cutting a length of paper the exact measurement of the circumference of the bottom edge of the frame.

Fold the paper in half, then in half again and continue folding until you have reduced the paper to about half the required width of a finished scallop.

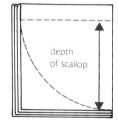 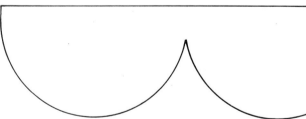

1 *Cut a pattern* △
Mark the depth of the scallop plus a 5mm seam allowance on to the folded paper and use a compass or a coin to draw a quarter-circle arc to the marked depth. Cut through all the layers of folded paper along this arc. Open up the paper carefully and you will have a row of even scallops which should fit the frame exactly.

Using the paper pattern, mark scallops on to the fabric by drawing neatly round the scalloped edge with a piece of tailor's chalk.

2 *Cut a scalloped edge* ◁
Add a 1cm seam allowance at each end of the trim before cutting out the fabric. Neaten the scalloped raw edges with zigzag stitch or blanket stitch and trim away any excess fabric.

Join the ends of the trim with a 1cm seam, press open and trim to match scallops if necessary. Fold the top seam allowance to the wrong side and attach trim to the fabric shade by topstitching along the marked straight edge.

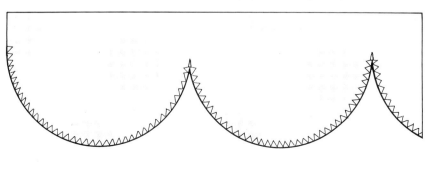

MAKING PLEATED LAMPSHADES

Lighting is an important feature in any room, so make your own shades to match your decorative scheme.

Lighting is one of the main aids to setting the atmosphere of a room, so it is worth paying some attention to the finish of your lampshades. Gently pleated lampshades are the perfect finishing touch in a softly decorated modern room, a cottagey room or a classically styled setting. By choosing fabrics and trimmings to tone or contrast with existing fabrics, you can achieve a well co-ordinated look at minimum cost.

Tailored, tightly stretched, waisted and shaped lampshades require practice and patience to perfect, but gathered or pleated shades with their softer finish are easier to make. The first thing you have to do when making up your own shades is to choose a frame in a shape to suit the style of your room. Then you have to bind the frame with tape, to give you a surface to which you can stitch the fabric you have chosen to cover the frame.

TOOLS AND EQUIPMENT

Lampshade frames Frames come in a wide range of sizes and shapes. This method of pleating the shade can be used to cover any strutted frame with straight or sloping sides. A straight drum-shape is quick and easy to cover. A coolie shade, where the top ring is much smaller then the bottom ring, looks particularly effective because the pleats fan out from the top. Do not use a frame with curved struts at the sides – this style must have straight struts.

Bear in mind that as well as looking at the shape of the frame, you must look at the fixing, to ensure that it will fit your lamp base or ceiling pendant. (Some shades are designed specifically for ceiling pendants.)

Tape is used to cover the lampshade frame so that the pleated fabric can be stitched directly to it. Buy straight cotton tape made specially for the purpose – it is 13mm wide, and you can easily dye it to tone with your fabric.

To find the total length of tape needed, measure all round the top and bottom rings of the shade, and along each strut (but not the struts which hold the shade to the light fitting). Multiply this figure by three.

You will also need pins, needles and sewing thread.

High, wide and handsome
Watered-silk-look fabric set in broad pleats makes a very effective shade for a classic ceramic lamp base. A bias trim in the same fabric adds an extra dimension to the pattern.

CHOOSE AND MEASURE

Choosing fabric Pleated shades should be made from fine fabrics such as chiffon, georgette, crepe, lawn or glazed cotton, that can easily be formed into pleats. Sheer fabric can be used if you back it with a lightweight woven interfacing, or use the fabric double so that the light bulb and frame will not show through.

To calculate the length For a drum-shaped shade, measure the circumference of one ring. Multiply this figure by three and add 10cm. For a coolie shade, measure the circumference of the larger bottom ring. Multiply this figure by 1½ and add 10cm.

If you have to use more than one width of fabric, allow an extra 5cm on each extra piece for joining up.

To calculate the depth measure along one strut and add 5cm.

Lightweight interfacing can be used to back thin fabric so that the frame will not show through. You will need a piece the same size as the fabric for the shade. Alternatively, for fine fabrics, double the length of fabric needed and work with double thickness.

Bias binding is a convenient method of trimming the top and bottom of the shade, or you can make your own bias fabric strips.

If you use bias binding, measure the circumference of the top and bottom rings, and cut a length to each measurement plus 3cm.

If you are making your own binding, cut bias strips (see page 37) 4cm wide and join them to make up lengths to fit the top and bottom rings, allowing 1.5cm for seams where necessary.

TAPING THE FRAME

The top and bottom rings of the frame, and each strut connecting them, must be taped as a base for stitching the fabric shade in place. Do not tape the struts which are for fixing the shade to the lamp base.

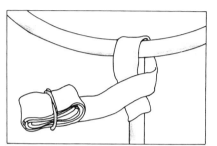

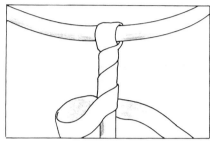

1 Prepare the tape
Measure the struts and, for each except one, cut a piece of tape three times the length. Then wind up the cut tape and secure it with a rubber band, leaving about 20cm loose from the bundle. This will stop it getting twisted as you work.

2 Start taping one strut △
Hold the loose end of tape against the top front of a strut so it hangs down the strut about 5mm. Take the bundle of tape up over the top ring, round behind and across the front to wrap over the loose end.

3 Finish taping the strut △
Work down the strut to the bottom ring, wrapping the tape diagonally so that it overlaps slightly. Make sure that it is wound smoothly and very tightly – if it is loose enough to twist on the metal, start again.

---

4 Secure the tape ▽
At the bottom of the strut, secure the tape by passing it round the bottom ring and back through the loop to make a knot. Pull the knot tight and leave the loose end of tape dangling.

Tape each of the struts except one using this method.

5 Prepare remaining tape
Measure the top and bottom rings, and the last untaped strut. Cut a piece of tape three times this length, and wind it up in a neat bundle, held with an elastic band as before.

6 Tape the top ring ▷
Hold the loose end of the tape against the top ring at the join with the untaped strut. Then wind the tape round to the inside of the ring and back over the ring again to wrap over and secure the loose end.

Then bind the top ring as on the struts, working right round to the untaped strut again.

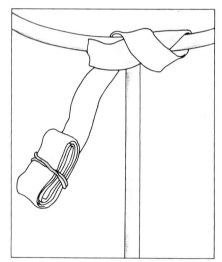

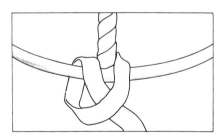

CHECK YOUR NEEDS
☐ Fabric
☐ Lampshade frame
☐ Lightweight interfacing (optional)
☐ Cotton tape, 13mm wide
☐ Tailor's chalk
☐ Dressmaking pins
☐ Sewing thread to match fabric
☐ Sewing needles
☐ Bias binding, 2.5cm wide (folded) OR 4cm wide bias strips cut from fabric for trimming.

7 Tape the bottom ring ▷
When you reach the untaped strut, wind the tape round it in a figure of eight and then tape down its length. At the bottom of the strut, wind the tape round in a figure of eight and start to work round the bottom ring in the same way as the top.

At each join between bottom ring and strut, trim the dangling surplus tape to leave a 1cm end and work the figure of eight over this end to secure it.

Trim the very end of the tape to 5mm. Turn under and stitch it neatly to the bound ring on the inside.

A PLEATED DRUM SHADE

A drum (or nearly drum-shaped) shade is the easiest shape to cover if you are not experienced.

1 *Cut out and prepare fabric*
The fabric should be three times the distance round the frame, by the depth of the frame, plus a 2.5cm seam allowance all round. For sheer fabrics, cut two layers of fabric, or one of fabric and one of lining, and tack together 3cm from raw edges all round.

Finish the side edges of the fabric, unless they are selvedges, with machine zigzag to prevent fraying. Top and bottom edges are left raw as they are neatened with bias binding.

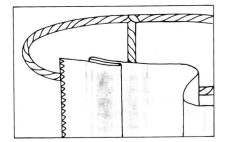

2 *Mark up pleats*
Measure the distance between two struts on the top ring and decide on a pleasing number of pleats to fit round this. It is a good idea to check the effect by pleating some of the fabric, as you may find some sizes of pleat suit the fabric better than others.

3 *Mark pleat positions* ▷
Using tailor's chalk, draw a line to mark a 1.5cm overlap allowance at the end of the fabric (this is tucked into the last pleat to give a neat finish). Then use chalk to mark out the pleat positions along top and bottom edges of fabric. For each pleat, mark its width, then twice its width for the underlap.

4 *Pin to the frame* ◁
Leaving the overlap allowance free, make the first pleat. (Keep the fold line straight with the grain of the fabric if it is a straight-sided drum shade.) Pin the pleat to the top ring so that the chalk line lies on a strut and the top edge of the pleat overlaps the ring by 2.5cm.

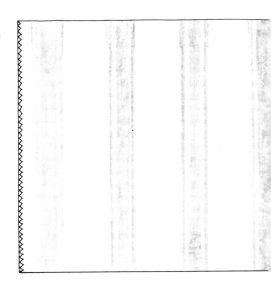

5 *Pin round the frame*
Pin the pleats into place around the top of the frame between the first two struts. Then pin round the lower edge of that section keeping the pleats taut, straight and even. Repeat for each section of the frame. If the lower ring is larger, adjust the pleats – see Pleated Coolie Shade (below).

6 *Tuck in raw edges* ◁
When you get to the point where the fabric meets, lap the last pleat over the raw edge you started with, arranging the fabric so that both the ends are tucked into pleats. Re-pin the first and last pleats if necessary to completely cover the frame.

7 *Stitch the fabric* ◁
Oversew all round the top of the frame from the outside, making sure each pleat is firmly stitched on to the taped ring and removing pins as you work. Repeat round the bottom ring.

8 *Trim seam allowance*
Trim off the surplus fabric from above the top ring and below the bottom ring, carefully cutting close to the stitching so that the fabric is flush with the frame. (See separate section overleaf for instructions for trimming the edge of the frame.)

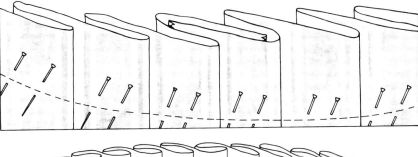

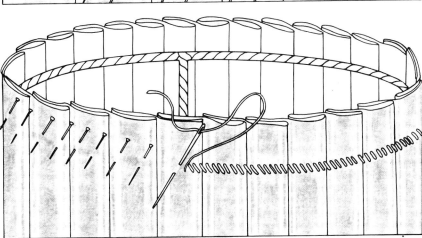

A PLEATED COOLIE SHADE

Working on a coolie shade is slightly different because of the size difference between top and bottom rings.

1 *Calculate amount of fabric*
To calculate the amount of fabric you need to cover the frame, measure around the bottom ring and multiply this figure by 1½. Measure a strut to give the depth of fabric. Add 2.5cm seam allowance all round and cut out.

2 *Calculate the size of the pleats*
Divide the length of the fabric by the circumference of the smaller ring to find out how much fullness each pleat must take up. For example, if the larger ring measures 100cm round, and the smaller ring measures 25cm round, each pleat has to take up six times the fullness of the fabric (i.e. the lower ring is 100cm, the fabric is 150cm long, and the pleating round the top of the frame must take up 150/25 = 6).

A good size of pleat in this case would be 5mm, with 2.5cm folded under each pleat. You will then be able to fit 50 pleats (150cm/3cm or 25cm/5mm) round the top of the frame.

The calculations may seem quite tricky, but you can experiment and adjust the size of the pleats and the fullness before the final stitching is done.

3 *Mark and fold the pleats* ▽
Work along the top edge of the fabric, first marking a 2.5cm seam allowance, then the width of the pleat, alternating with the underlap allowance of the pleat.

Fold up the pleats and pin in place to ensure that your calculations were accurate and the fabric fits neatly round the top.

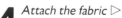

4 *Attach the fabric* ▷
Working on one section of the shade at a time, pin the fabric in place. Pin along the top, from one strut to the next, holding the pleats neatly, then stretch the fabric down in line with the struts and pin the fabric to the lower ring, ensuring the fullness is distributed evenly.

Tuck under seam allowance at the ends of the fabric. Stitch to the rings and trim away seam allowance as for a drum-shaped shade.

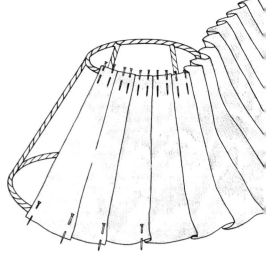

TRIMMING THE SHADE
All that remains is to neaten the edges of the shade where you have trimmed the fabric away.

1 *Prepare to trim*
Press 5mm to the wrong side, down each long edge of bias strip (this may be pre-pressed on purchased binding). With wrong sides together, fold the bias binding in half along its length and press.

2 *Attach the trim* ▷
Open out the binding and pin to the shade round upper and lower edges with the right side of the binding facing the right side of the shade. The binding should be positioned so that the raw edge of the binding is close to the raw edge of the lampshade fabric and the first fold line is just below the line of stitches attaching the fabric to the frame. Sew in place using a stab stitch (stab the needle through the binding and the shade fabric, draw the needle through, then stab the needle back through the shade and the binding, taking just a very small stitch each time).

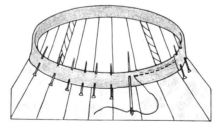

3 *Finish the trim* ▷
Fold the binding over the top of the shade (or the bottom of the shade) and slipstitch it in place stitching just inside the previous row of stitches. Finally neaten the ends: cut one at a 45° angle, turn under and lap over the other one. Secure with small stitches.

Low, soft and charming △
A coolie-shaped shade in a fine, softly pleated fabric makes the perfect partner for a spherical base.

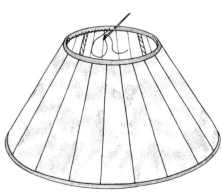

BRIGHT IDEA

Loosely fitted shade For a soft effect, with a minimum of sewing, make a coolie shade which is fitted to the top ring only. Cut the fabric 1 ½ times the circumference of the lower ring, plus 1.5cm seam allowance, at each end, by the depth of the frame plus a total of 7.5cm seam allowance.

Join the two short edges with a flat seam, right sides together. Hem the lower edge. Bind only the top ring of the lampshade frame, and attach the fabric as described in Step 4 above, round the top of the frame only. Adjust the size of the pleats to take up all the fullness if necessary. The fabric can then be left to fall over the lower ring of the frame.

MAKING YOUR OWN LOOSE COVERS – 1

Loose covers for chairs or sofas can give a room a whole new look. Start with simple shapes and clever ideas.

Traditional tailored loose covers are not as difficult to make as you might think. They are pieced and pinned together on the chair itself, rather like dressmaking on a tailor's dummy. This gives you plenty of opportunity to adjust the shape and fit, before you actually stitch the cover.

However, fitted loose covers do involve a fair amount of sewing. Use good quality fabrics, or you may find that having spent days stitching a cover, it wears out after a couple of years. So rather than start with an intricate shape, in this chapter we look at two ideas for simple but stylish loose covers, before

going on to larger pieces of furniture.

If you're not very experienced, it would be a good idea to start by making some gusseted cushions (see Simple Gusseted Cushions). The techniques used to make these uniform shapes are adapted to make full covers. For tied-on styles, try wrapping old pieces of sheeting round the chair or sofa to test the effect and help give you an idea of the amount of fabric needed before you buy.

FABRICS AND FASTENINGS

Avoid heavy fabrics, as some of the seams will have up to four layers of fabric, plus piping, which may be heavy going on a standard sewing machine. Furnishing cottons and linen unions are usually the most suitable choices – although you can use finer fabrics for occasional furniture which does not get so much wear.

Fastenings Because the covers fit tightly, they may have to have fastenings – usually down one of the back corner seams. These may be hook-and-eye tapes or zips. For the simpler, softer styles in this chapter, use Velcro or fabric ties. Covers are usually tied under the furniture too, with tapes running through casings.

Measuring up Before calculating how much fabric you need, you will have to measure up the chair or sofa. Decide where the seams should go and what type of opening you want to make. Then measure each section of the chair and add 5cm in each direction, taking the maximum measurement where sections have curved seams. You can use the seams on the existing fitted (usually calico) cover as a guide. If the chair or sofa already has a loose cover, you can use this as a pattern.

CHECK YOUR NEEDS
☐ Tape measure
☐ Pencil and paper
☐ Ruler
☐ Dressmaker's chalk
☐ Scissors
☐ Pins and needles
☐ Fabric for cover
☐ Piping cord
☐ Contrast fabric for pleats, piping and ties (optional)
☐ Sewing machine
☐ Thread

Pretty well dressed
This upholstered dining chair is softened with cover, skirt, and contrasting bows in glazed cotton. Adapt the technique for other shapes.

MEASURING UP

The first thing to do is to decide on the positions of the seams and measure up the chair. Here we show how to measure and cut out panels for a dining chair with an upholstered back and seat. The technique can be adapted for other shapes and styles of chair.

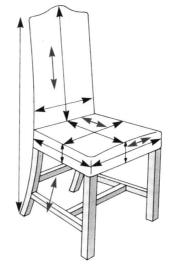
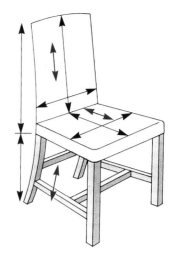

1 *Measuring up* ▷
Measure each section at its maximum height, depth or width, adding 5cm in each direction for seam allowances. In some designs, you will also need to add an allowance for tuck-ins if the cover tucks into a deep crack between back and seat. Allow an extra 15cm along any edge which has to be tucked in.

2 *Plan a cutting layout* ▷
Decide on the fabric you are going to use, and draw up a scale drawing, showing the width of the fabric with two parallel lines. Sketch in the various panels of fabric, ensuring that they lie along the straight grain of the fabric as indicated.

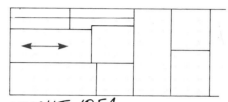
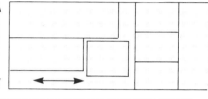

3 *Calculate fabric*
When you are happy with the layout, calculate how much fabric you will need. If you want to pipe any of the seams, work out how much piping and bias-cut fabric for binding you will need.

BRIGHT IDEA

Casual approach If you can't face intricate sewing, cover a chair with the ultimate loose cover: a length of fabric, thrown over the existing cover. Choose a bold pattern for drama or a plain fabric for a more subtle effect. Neaten the edges and tuck the fabric firmly into the angles between the seat, arms and back to anchor it.

SLIPOVER COVER WITH SKIRT

These instructions are for a cover for an upholstered, armless chair, like the one shown on the previous page: they could equally well apply to a hardbacked chair with an upholstered seat. A simple, gathered skirt and bows down each side to tie the cover in place give an informal finish. Measure up and cut out all panels except the skirt.

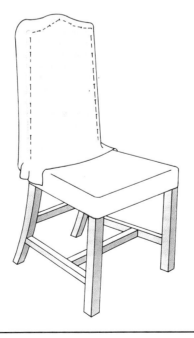
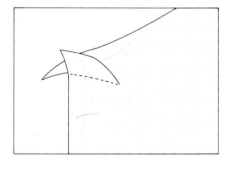

1 *Fit front panel* ▷
Lay the front panel centrally on the back of the chair, pinning it in place with the right side of the fabric facing the chair. Use dressmaker's chalk to mark seamlines. Leave a generous (15cm) seam allowance at the lower edge, where the cover tucks in to the crease between the back and seat of the chair.

2 *Take in fullness* △
At the top corners, if there is not a gusset round the chair back, you may need to take in fullness for a neat fit. Make a small dart, with the point at the front corner of the back of the chair, pinning it so that the stitching line lies along the angle of the corner. Make and pin any other pleats and tucks necessary for a good fit.

3 *Fit the back panel*
Position the back panel on the back of the chair, with the right side of the fabric facing the chair, so that the edges of the panel match the edges of the front panel. Pin the panels together down the sides and across the top, following the chalked seamlines.

4 *Tack and stitch*
Tack the darts and stitch. Press to one side, towards the centre back of the chair. Tack any other pleats and tucks. Pin piping into curved top seam, then tack and stitch seam. Neaten seam allowances together and press towards the back panel.

5 *Seat panel*
Lay the seat panel on the seat, right side facing chair, and mark the seamline round the edge of the chair with chalk.

6 *Gusset pieces* ▷
Pin seat gusset pieces round sides and front of seat, with right side of fabric facing seat, pinning seamlines at front corners to match front corners of seat panel. Tack and stitch seams at corners of gusset. Press seams open.

7 *Position seat section*
Re-position seat section and joined gusset pieces round sides and front of seat, right side of gusset facing chair. Pin gusset sections to seat section, ensuring the seamlines match the corners of the seat panel.

8 *Check fit* ▷
Before stitching gusset to seat, slip the back section over the back of the chair, inside out, and pin lower edge of front panel of back cover to back edge of seat panel. Where the seam at the back of the seat meets the gusset/seat seam, mark the top edge of the gusset (see arrow). Beyond this point, pin the top edge of the gusset to the front panel of the back of the chair.

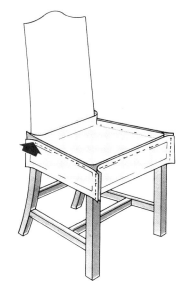

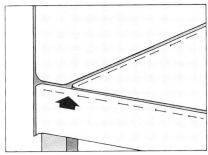

9 *Seat seams*
When you are happy with the fit, insert piping round top of gusset (allowing sufficient piping to reach to the back edge). Tack and stitch the seam round the top of the gusset, stitching as far as the marked points only (see arrow). Clip seam allowance across corners, trim and press towards gusset. Stitch the piping to the top edge of the gusset from marked point to the back of the seat on each side.

10 *Join back section to seat*
Fit the sections on the chair again and re-pin the seam along the back of the seat. You may need to trim away some of the 15cm seam allowance at each side of the back seat seam. Pin the seam in a gentle curve, so that there is a tongue to tuck into the angle of the seat. Tack and stitch seam, then neaten seam allowances together. Pin, tack and stitch front panel to top of gusset from marked point to back, clipping into seam allowances. Neaten seam allowances and press towards gusset.

11 *Side openings* ▷
Slip cover on to chair and fold back seam allowance along marked fold lines down the side openings. Fold back ends of gusset in line with upper part of side openings. Mark points for attaching ties spaced evenly down each side of each opening.

12 *Make up ties*
For each tie, cut a strip of fabric 7cm by 30cm. Fold in half along length, right sides together, and stitch across one short end and down one long edge, taking 1.5cm seam allowances. Turn right side out.

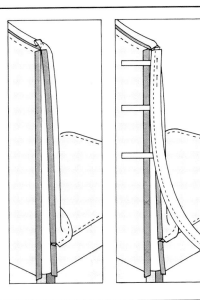

13 *Finish opening edges*
Pin ties to front and back panels at each marked point. Pin piping down each opening edge of front panel so that stitching line of piping meets marked fold line. At top of opening, trim piping cord away and fold piping under for a neat finish. Tack and stitch piping in place through seam allowance of front panel, enclosing ends of ties as you stitch. Stitch ties to seam allowance of back panel. Press seam allowances of piping and front panel away from opening, trim and neaten seam allowances together. Press seam allowance of back panel towards opening, so it can be tucked inside front panel. Neaten raw edge.

14 *Make up skirt*
For the back skirt, measure the width of the lower edge of the back panel from the neatened edge of one seam allowance to the other. Multiply this measurement by 1.5, add 3cm seam allowances, and cut a panel to this measurement by the depth of the skirt, plus 5cm hem allowance and 1.5cm seam allowance. Measure round the lower edge of gusset, round sides and front, from piping down back openings. Multiply by 1.5 and add 3cm seam allowance to find length of skirt section. Cut out panel, joining widths if necessary. Turn under 5mm then 1cm down each side edge of each skirt section and stitch. Run two lines of gathering stitches round top of skirt sections.

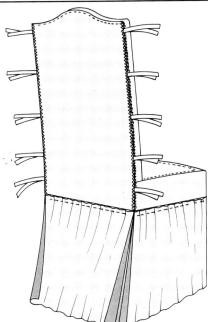

15 *Attach skirt* ◁
Slip cover over chair, inside out. Draw up skirt sections to fit. Pin skirt panels to lower edge of gusset round sides and front of chair and to lower edge of back panel, distributing fullness evenly. Insert piping into seam before tacking and stitching. Neaten seam allowances together and press towards gusset. With cover in position, mark hemline. Turn up and stitch 1cm round lower edge of hem, then turn up hem along foldline and slipstitch in place.

PLEATED SKIRTS

These covers have inverted pleats in a contrast fabric down the centre of the back and at each front corner of the chair. Piping round the edge of the seat is in the same fabric as the pleats.

1 Measure up and cut out
Measure up as before. Cut out panels 5cm larger in each direction, allowing 15cm for the tuck-in at the back of the seat and the bottom of the front panel. For the back panel, add 3cm to the width measurement, to insert the inverted pleat. Prepare piping.

2 Cut out pleat fabric
For the centre back pleat, cut a panel the same height as the back panel and 35cm wide. For the corner pleats, cut two panels the same height as the skirt sections, and 35cm wide.

3 Make up back panel ▷
Cut the back panel in half down its length. With right sides together and raw edges matching, join each long edge of the pleat fabric to each side of the back panel, taking 1.5cm seams. Press seam and neaten seam allowances together.

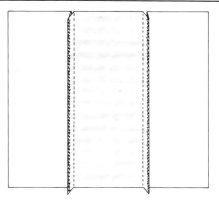

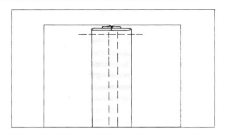

4 Fold pleat △
With wrong sides facing, fold pleated section in half so that seam lines match. Tack together down seam lines.

5 Re-fold inverted pleat ▷
Open out on a flat surface so that right side of the back panel pieces face down. Press pleat so that it is flat against the back panel with the centre of the pleat matching the seam lines which are tacked together. Tack pleat in place at top edge. Make two lines of tacking

stitches down centre of pleat, close to and on each side of tacked seamline, stitching through to right sides of back panel sections. From right side, stitch pleat in place, topstitching from top of back panel to halfway down the back panel, at approximately seat level.

6 Make up skirt section ◁
Trim side edges of front skirt so it is 3cm wider than the finished measurement. Join contrast pleat panels and set pleats in place at the corner seams, as for back panel, topstitching the pleat in place for just 15cm down from top edge.

7 Make up cover
Pin and tack the remaining seams in the following order, fitting the pieces on the chair as before. Join seat panel to pleated skirt panels at sides and front, inserting piping. Join lower edge of front panel to back of seat panel, shaping the tuck-in allowance to fit down between the front and back sections. Finally, join back panel to rest of seat, down sides and across top edge. Pin and tack before stitching to ensure that the cover will slip on and off easily. If necessary, put a zip or Velcro fastening into one side opening.

8 Hem and buttons
Unpick tacking down pleat openings. Fit cover on chair, right side out, and mark hemline. Turn up 1cm all round and stitch, then turn up hem and slipstitch in place. (You will get a neater effect if you unpick the last few centimetres of the pleat seams and stitch the hem of each panel of the skirt separately, then re-stitch seams.) Stitch a button in place on either side of the centre back pleat, to strengthen the seam at the top of the pleat.

◁ **Italian style**
Slick colours and simple lines give these slipover covers with inverted pleats instant pzazz.

MAKING LOOSE COVERS – 2

From gusseted cushions and slipover covers for upholstered dining chairs it is a simple step to full loose covers.

Loose covers have a great many advantages over tight, permanently fixed covers for upholstered furniture. The first is that they can be washed or dry cleaned regularly, which not only keeps them looking better, but helps them to wear better too. You can have new covers made up when old ones become worn or when you want to change your colour scheme, and you can even go as far as having two sets of covers, to give your room a different look for winter and summer months.

Professionally-made covers are expensive, and there seem to be fewer and fewer local seamstresses who are prepared to make up covers and curtains for a reasonable sum. So if you have simply-shaped chairs and sofas and a little experience of home sewing it is worth making your own.

TRIMS AND FINISHES

Piping Most covers look smarter if the seams are piped: contrast piping gives a crisp finish, but it is probably better to use the same fabric for the cover and the piping if you are not experienced – this will help to disguise wobbly seams and uneven stitching.

Use no. 5 piping cord covered in 3.5cm wide bias-cut binding.

Skirts The lower edge of the cover may be finished simply with a drawstring to pull the edges under the piece of furniture. However, for a smarter finish, a straight skirt with inverted pleats at the corners or a box-pleated skirt may be added. For a softer finish with a country cottage appeal, add a gathered skirt. Complement the finish with scatter cushions trimmed to match.

Closures Traditionally, hook and eye tape was used to hold loose covers tightly closed. This was a closely woven cotton tape in two halves – one with hooks and the other with eyelets or bars to match. Now Velcro is the most popular choice, but you can also use popper tape (similar to hook and eye tape, but with press studs) or zips (choose a medium weight nylon one).

CHOOSE YOUR FABRICS

Tightly-woven furnishing cottons and linen unions are the best choice for loose covers. Look out for fabric which has been treated to resist stains – this is certainly an advantage for the first couple of years of the cover's life. If you want a patterned fabric (which will help to disguise any defects in your sewing and irregularities in the seam lines) try to use all-over patterns, rather than large motifs with borders: these need clever planning and careful positioning to be effective. It is also worth bearing in mind that the larger the pattern is, the more fabric you will need to get accurate positioning of pattern motifs.

SOFAS AND CHAIRS

The general techniques for sofas and chairs are similar. The main difference is that sofas are generally wider than the width of the fabric, so you have to join pieces of fabric to make up some of the panels for the cover. Position a full width of fabric in the *centre* of the sofa (inner and outer back panels, seat and front seat panel) and join small sections to each side to make up the width.

A tight fit
Smart fitted covers show off the simple lines of this sofa. The shape is further emphasized by inserting contrast piping along the main seam lines and round the gusseted cushions.

MEASURING UP

The first thing is to measure up the sofa or chair and decide on seam lines. The tight (usually calico) cover should give you a guide – or follow the existing loose cover if you are replacing it. See overleaf for details of allowances for skirts.

I	Inner back
2	Outer back
·	(behind sofa)
3	Seat
4	Front seat
5	Outer arm
6	Inner arm
7	Arm gusset

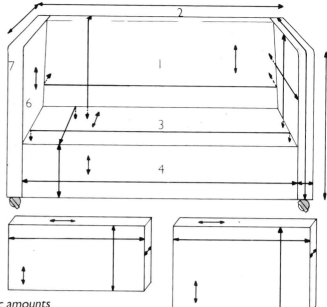

1 *Measure at maximum points ▷*
Divide the chair or sofa into sections, marking seam lines on the existing cover if necessary. Measure each section at its maximum depth, width or height. Measure up seat and back cushions as for gusseted cushions (see page 72). The red arrows indicate direction of grain, and blue lines indicate seams to be piped.

Back and seat cushions made up from back and front panels and gusset sections

2 *Add seam allowances*
To give you plenty of spare fabric, so you can adjust the fit of the cover, add 10cm for seam allowances to each dimension. Along the sides and back of the seat there is generally a crack, into which you tuck the seam of the cover so to anchor it. Allow an extra 15cm along any of the edges of the panels that are going to tuck in (usually the back and lower edge of the inner arm panels, the side and lower edges of the inner back panel and the side and back edges of the seat panel). Allow 20cm all along lower edges of back, outer sides and front of seat for making a casing and drawing the cover tight under the sofa.

3 *Calculate fabric amounts*
On graph paper, make a scale drawing to give you a cutting layout. Start by drawing parallel lines to represent the selvedges of the fabric, and sketch in rectangles to represent the sections of the cover. If the fabric is patterned, mark the repeat along one edge of the diagram, so you can position the panels appropriately. When the layout is right calculate the amount of fabric. Allow extra for bias strips if needed.

4 *Measure for closure*
Measure the back outside corner of the sofa to give you the length of Velcro or other fastening required.

CHECK YOUR NEEDS
☐ Tape measure
☐ Pencil and ruler
☐ Paper and graph paper
☐ Dressmaker's chalk
☐ Pins and needles
☐ Fabric for cover
☐ Piping cord (optional)
☐ Contrast fabric for piping (optional)
☐ Bias binding
☐ Zip, Velcro or hook and eye tape, as necessary
☐ Scissors

MAKING THE COVER

Here we give instructions for making a cover in plain fabric (with contrast piping, to make the diagrams easier to follow). The shape is a simple, squared sofa: the seams in the first step are usually unnecessary for a chair. The cover is held firmly under the chair with a casing and drawstring.

1 *Join fabric to make up panels*
Cut out fabric, following the cutting layout you sketched when calculating fabric amounts. The inner back, outer back, seat and front seat sections usually need extra seams. Use full widths of fabric for the centre of each of these panels, with pieces joined to each side to make up the width.

2 *Make up piping*
Cut out 3.5cm wide bias strips, joining lengths as necessary to make up a series of strips to fit round all the seams which are to be piped. Use the strips to cover size 5 piping cord. You will need a fair amount if the sofa or chair has extra cushions – it does help to make it all up before you start.

3 *Join back and seat panels ◁*
Position the inner and outer back panels on the sofa, wrong side out, pinning each piece to the sofa and marking seam lines with dressmaker's chalk. Pin seam lines to check fit, and take in any fullness with small tucks if the back of the sofa is curved, or with a neat dart if necessary at angular corners. Position the seat panel and front seat panel and pin in the same way, leaving a 15cm tuck-in allowance along the back seat seam. When you are happy with the fit, remove the panels, trim seams to exactly 1.5cm and insert piping where necessary. Tack and stitch seams and neaten seam allowances.

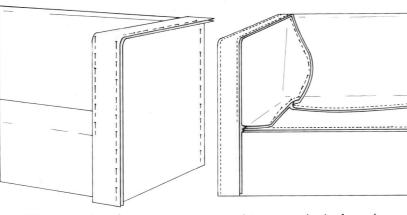

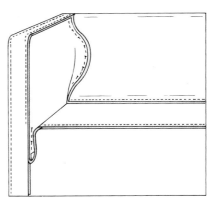

4 *Join arm sections* △
For each arm, pin sections to arms of chair, wrong sides out, and mark seam lines. Position gusset along top of arm and down front of arm. Mark and pin seams as before. Remove arm sections, trim seam allowances, insert piping, tack, stitch seams and neaten seam allowances as before.

5 *Join arms to back of seat* △
Re-position the back and seat section and the arms on the sofa, inside out, and pin seams down the inner back corners. This seam will have to be shaped, with a 15cm tuck-in allowance at the lowest point, tapering to give a neat fit at the top where the inner back panel meets the piping at the top of the inner arm. Pin sides of seat to lower edge of inner arm, with tuck-in allowance. Mark seam lines.

6 *Join front seat to arms* △
With the pieces still in position inside-out on the sofa, tuck the 15cm allowance into the crease down each side of the seat. Pin the front edge of the tuck-in at the side of the seat section to the side edge of the front panel. Pin the remaining side edge of the front panel to the inner edge of the front arm gusset section. Mark seam lines.

7 *Mark back seam lines*
Pin outer back to arm gussets at each side, and pin sides of outer back to outer arms down each corner seam line. Mark seam lines.

8 *Stitch seams*
When you are happy with the fit, remove cover, trim seam allowances accurately, insert piping, and tack (apart from down one back corner where closure is to be inserted). Stitch seams and neaten seam allowances.

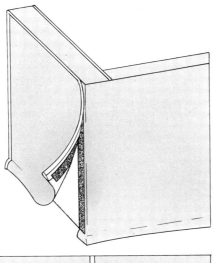

9 *Finish back opening* ◁
Turn under 5mm then 1cm down opening edge of outer back panel. Turn under 5mm down opening edge of outer arm panel. Press under along marked seam line. Pin piping down opening edge of outer arm panel, matching stitching of piping to marked seam line. Tack and stitch in place.
Pin and tack Velcro in place down each opening edge. Topstitch across the top of the opening so that neatened seam allowances are pressed away from back. Alternatively, set zip, hook and eye or popper tape into opening down outer back corner.

10 *Fit round legs* ◁
Fit cover on to sofa, inside out, and trim away fabric for a neat fit round the legs, leaving a 1cm seam allowance. Neaten the raw edge with bias binding, stitching the binding to the raw edge with a 1cm seam, then turning binding and seam allowance to inside and slipstitch folded edge in place.

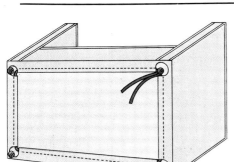

11 *Make casing* ◁
You will now have four flaps, which have to be drawn together to hold the cover in place. Turn under 1cm along each of the four long raw edges, then turn under a further 2cm. Pin, tack and stitch to make a casing. Measure each channel, and cut a length of tape to this length plus about 70cm. Thread tape through each casing in turn, starting from opening corner.

12 *Make up cushion covers*
Make up piped, gusseted cushion covers for any back and seat cushions which form part of the sofa or chair, following instructions in Simple Gusseted Cushions. Position zips in one of the gusset panels (the back panel for the seat cushions and the lower edge panel for the back cushions), so that they cannot be seen when the cushions are in position, and the cushions are therefore reversible.

ADDING A SKIRT
Start by making up the cover: this is measured exactly as for the detailed example, but omitting the 20cm allowance round the lower edge of the front seat, front and outer arms and outer back panels. Make up as far as the end of step 8.

1 Mark skirt seam line ▷
Put the cover on the sofa right side out and mark a line for the top of the skirt. The height of the line will depend on the proportions of the sofa (or chair) but about 15cm is a good depth. Measure round sofa at marked line. Trim cover 2cm below marked line.

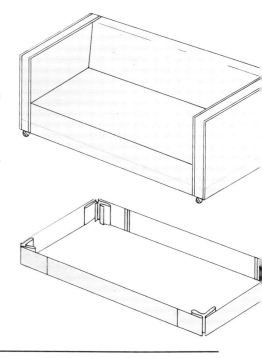

2 Calculate length of skirt
For a pleated skirt, allow three times the measurement round the chair, plus 1.5cm seam allowance at each end. For a gathered skirt, allow 1½ times the measurement, plus seam allowances. For a straight skirt with inverted pleats, add 30cm for each of the four pleats plus seam allowances. Measure from the marked line to the floor and add 3cm for the depth.

3 Cut out fabric for skirt ▷
Cut out strips of fabric to make up the skirt to the appropriate dimensions. Join strips. Where possible position seams inside pleats. For a straight skirt, position seams in the straight front and back sections of the skirt to match up with seam lines down seat front and outer back panels of sofa. Prepare sufficient piping to go all round marked line if required.

4 Cut out flaps
Measure the length of each lower edge of the sofa and subtract 15cm from each measurement. Measure from the marked line round the cover to 10cm under the sofa. Add 4.5cm. For each lower edge, cut a strip to these measurements to form a flap to go under the sofa to hold it in place.

5 Make up skirt
Turn under 5mm then 1cm down short ends of skirt and along lower raw edge. Gather or pleat skirt, pinning and tacking to hold in place (see page 90, for details of how to make an inverted pleat). At the opening corner, make half the inverted pleat at each end of the skirt.

6 Piping and flaps
Stitch piping to right side of gathered or pleated edge, with raw edges of piping towards raw edge of skirt, turning under piping at ends.
Turn under and stitch 5mm then 1cm down each short edge of flaps. Turn under 1cm then 2cm down one long edge of each flap. Stitch to form casings.

7 Attach skirt and flaps ▷ ▷
Remove cover from sofa. Pin skirt to right side of cover, with raw edge of skirt just inside neatened edge of cover, right sides facing, so that piping is sandwiched between skirt and cover. The stitching line of the piping should match the marked line round the cover. Pin flaps in place so that raw edge of flap matches raw edge of skirt, with right side of flap facing wrong side of skirt. Tack through all layers. Stitch in place and press seam allowances upwards and skirt and flaps

downwards.
Finish the cover by fitting Velcro down the opening edges and making up gusseted cushions as before.

▽ Patterns for camouflage
A fabric with an all-over pattern in soft tones of cream, beige and peach has many advantages: it disguises irregularities in seam lines and helps to mask stains and spills.

BRIGHT IDEA

Extra protection It is a good idea to use remnants of fabric to make arm covers, as the arms get a lot of wear and tear. The seam lines of the protectors should follow the seam lines of the cover. Make up the protectors as large as possible, preferably the same depth as the arm, and the same height as the inner arm, so that they can tuck down beside the seat cushion. To hold the protectors in place, stitch a small hook to each corner and make a hand-sewn bar on the cover for the hook to catch in.

INDEX

PHOTOGRAPHIC CREDITS
Front cover Sunway Blinds, 1 Kingfisher Wallcoverings by Nairn, 2-3 EWA/Rodney Hyett, 4-5 Kingfisher Wallcoverings by Nairn, 6 Next Interior, 7 National Magazine Company/David Allen, 9 Curtain Net Advisory Bureau, 11 Arthur Sanderson and Sons, 14 Jan Baldwin/Eaglemoss, 15 & 18 Curtain Net Advisory Bureau, 19 Harrison Drape, 22 Jan Baldwin/Eaglemoss, 23 Arthur Sanderson and Sons, 26 Jerry Tubby/Eaglemoss, 27 Syndication International, 30 The Picture Library, 31 Swish, 34 Textra, 35 Ruflette, 39 EWA, 41 Curtain Net Advisory Bureau, 42 Crown Wallcoverings, 53 Sunway Blinds, 56 Michael Boys, 57 Habitat, 59 Arthur Sanderson and Sons, 61 EWA/Michael Nicholson, 63 Curtain Net Advisory Bureau, 64 EWA/Michael Dunne, 67 Designers Guild, 71 Sara Taylor/Eaglemoss, 74 Dorma, 75 EWA/Jerry Tubby, 76 Jerry Tubby/Eaglemoss, 79, 81, 83, 86 Jan Baldwin/Eaglemoss, 87 & 88 Syndication International, 90 PWA International, 91 & 94 Tulleys of Chelsea

ILLUSTRATIONS
David Ashby (Garden Studios), Craig Austin (Garden Studios), Lindsay Blow, Terence Evans, John Hutchinson, Kevin Jones Associates, Coral Mula, Fraser Newman, Stan North, Adam Willis

Contents

Words shown in **bold** in the text are explained in the glossary.

The download button shows there are free worksheets or other resources available. Go to:

www.rubytuesdaybooks.com/scienceKS1

Autumn Acorns

It's autumn in a park.

Squirrel

A squirrel is eating acorns that drop from oak trees.

Acorn

The squirrel buries some of the acorns in the ground.

FUNdamental
Science
0 1 2 3 4 5 6 7 8 9 10 11 12 13 14 15 16 17 18 19 20
Key Stage 1

From a Tiny Seed to a Mighty Tree

How Plants Grow

by Ruth Owen

Ruby Tuesday Books

Published in 2016 by Ruby Tuesday Books Ltd.

Editor: Mark J. Sachner
Designer: Emma Randall
Consultant: Judy Wearing, PhD, BEd
Production: John Lingham

Photo credits:
Alamy: 9 (bottom left), 22 (top); FLPA: 22 (bottom), 23 (bottom); Istock Photo: 29 (centre); Shutterstock: Cover, 1, 2–3, 4–5, 6–7, 8–9, 10–11, 12–13, 14–15, 16–17, 18–19, 20–21, 23 (top), 24–25, 26–27, 30–31.

British Library Cataloguing in Publication Data (CIP) is available for this title.

ISBN 978-1-910549-77-3

Printed in China by Toppan Leefung

www.rubytuesdaybooks.com

When winter comes, there is not much food around.

The squirrel digs up some of her buried acorns and eats them.

She doesn't find all the acorns, though....

Let's Talk

What do you think might happen to the acorns that stay buried in the ground?

5

A New Oak Tree

The buried acorns wait for winter to end.

In spring, the sunshine warms up the soil.

Under the ground, a tiny **shoot** sprouts from an acorn.

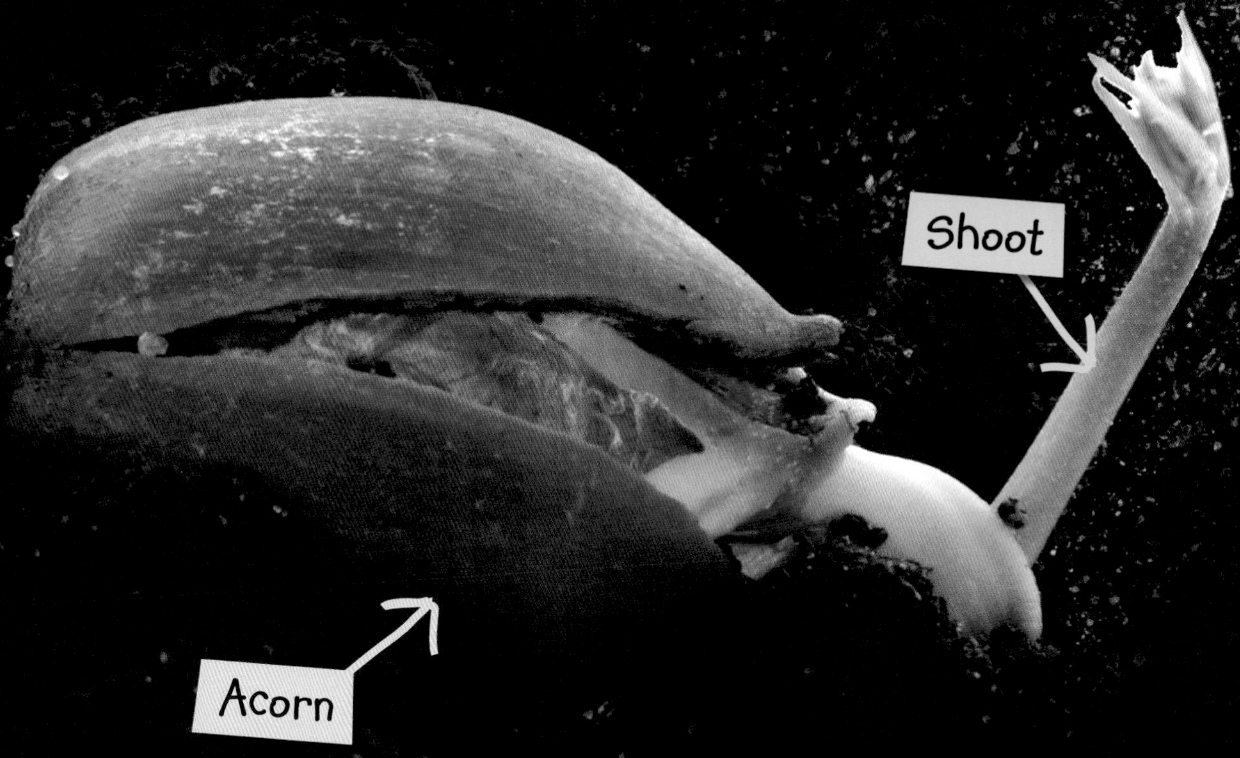

Shoot

Acorn

Inside an acorn there is an oak tree seed. The seed contains all the material needed to grow a new tree.

Oak tree seedling

Leaf

The shoot pushes up through the soil and into the sunshine.

After a few weeks, the shoot has grown into an oak tree **seedling** with **roots**, a stem and leaves.

Stem

The seedling takes in water from the soil through its roots.

Roots

Growing and Changing

The years go by and the little oak tree seedling grows.

Its stem becomes a thick trunk with long branches.

Branch

Trunk

When it is about 50 years old,
the tree begins to grow acorns.

An Oak Tree's Life Cycle

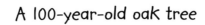

A 100-year-old oak tree

An oak tree may live for hundreds of years.

The story of how a living thing grows and changes is called its life cycle.

An acorn drops from the tree and grows in the soil.

A 50-year-old oak tree

After one year, the seedling is 0.5 m tall.

A seedling grows from the acorn.

Growing Sunflowers

A tree may take many years to grow from a seed. Other plants, such as sunflowers, grow in just a few months.

Sunflower

Sunflower seeds

Seeds contain a store of food. Seedlings use this food to help them grow.

A Sunflower's Life Cycle

A person plants a seed in soil in spring.

After four weeks a seedling grows.

The seedling gets taller and grows leaves.

In early summer, a flower bud forms.

The bud becomes a flower.

In late summer, seeds form in the centre of the flower – ready to make new plants next spring.

Let's Draw It!

Draw the life cycle of a sunflower.

Use the pictures on this page to help you.

Add these labels to your drawing.

Seed   **Seedling**   **Leaf**   **Bud**   **Flower**

Animal Helpers

Flowers produce a dust called **pollen** that is needed for making seeds.

Many plants need pollen from another plant of the same kind before they can produce seeds.

How does pollen get from one flower to another?

Lily flower

Petal

Pollen dust

When a bee visits a flower, pollen sticks to its body.

Then the bee carries the pollen to the flowers of another plant.

Now those flowers can produce seeds.

It's not just **insects** that help carry pollen from flower to flower. Birds, bats, lizards and many other animals also do this.

Honeybee

Pollen

Let's Talk

Why do you think bees, butterflies and other insects visit flowers?

A Flower's Sweet Treat

Flowers produce a sweet liquid called **nectar**.

Bees, butterflies and other animals visit flowers to feed on nectar.

Let's Talk

Honeybees carry some nectar and pollen back to their hives. Why do you think they do this?

(The answer is at the bottom of the page.)

Answer: Inside their hives, honeybees turn nectar into honey. They eat honey in winter when there are no flowers around. Bees feed pollen to their young.

A butterfly feeding on nectar

A flower's smell and colourful petals tell insects that there is nectar inside.

Be a Scientist!

On a warm, dry spring or summer day go bee watching in a garden or park.

1. Count the number of bees on each type of plant.

What colour flowers are the most popular?

Do the popular flowers have a strong smell?

2. Use a watch or phone to time a bee for one minute.

How many flowers does the bee visit in that time?

3. Use a magnifying glass to look closely at the flowers.

Do you observe any sticky nectar or dusty pollen inside?

BE CAREFUL!
Go bee watching with an adult. Do not disturb the bees. Do not touch the bees or put your face close to them.

All About Seeds

Seeds form inside protective coverings.

Apple tree seeds and tomato plant seeds are surrounded by soft fruits.

Seed

Apple

A tomato plant

Seeds form inside a flower.

A soft fruit forms around the seeds.

The fruit becomes a fat, red tomato.

Tomato plant seeds

Sunflower seed

Shell

Sunflower seeds have a hard shell.

Poppy seeds form inside a hard pod.

Poppy

Seedpod

Seeds

Spiky casing

The seeds of a horse chestnut tree are known as conkers. They grow inside spiky casings.

Seed

Cones and Seeds

Some plants, such as pine trees, don't grow flowers. Instead, they produce cones.

Some of a pine tree's cones release pollen into the air.

Pollen cone

Pollen

Scots pine tree

Other cones produce seeds.

Seed cone

Once pollen lands on the seed cones, seeds begin to form.

When the seeds are fully formed, the cone's woody scales open to release the seeds into the air.

Scales

The seed cone turns brown.

Seed

Be a Scientist!

Pine tree seeds must be released in dry weather so they can float in the air. If it is rainy or the air is damp, the seeds won't float. Let's investigate cones and seeds!

Gather your equipment:
- A cone with open scales
- A jar with a lid
- Water
- A notebook and pen

How does a cone stop its seeds being released in wet weather? Write your ideas in a notebook.

1. Put the cone in the jar.

2. Fill the jar with water so the cone is covered. Screw the lid on tight and leave for several hours.

What do you observe happens? Record the results in your notebook. Did the results match your ideas?

3. Next, remove the cone from the jar and place it somewhere warm.

What do you think will happen now?

What Do Seedlings Need?

Seedlings need a place to grow where there is soil, water, **nutrients** and sunshine.

Seedlings may struggle to grow if they are too close to their parent plant and other seedlings.

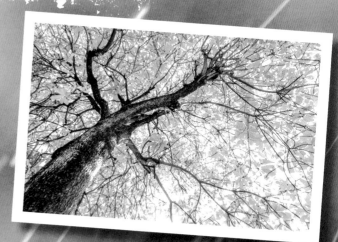

Seedling

The parent plant may block out sunlight.

Soil

There may not be enough water and nutrients in the soil for all the plants.

It's important that seedlings have space to grow away from their parent plant and each other.

Too crowded!

If too many seedlings try to grow in the same spot many of the little plants will die.

Space to grow!

Let's Talk

How do you think a plant spreads its seeds to new growing places?

Seeds on the Move

Many plants get help from animals to spread their seeds to new growing places. How?

Bramble plant

A fox eating blackberries

Animals eat berries and other fruit that contain seeds.

An animal's body digests the soft fruit but the hard seeds pass through.

The seeds leave the animal's body in its poo — often far from the parent plant!

Fox poo containing bramble seeds

Seeds

Some seeds have hooks and hairs that attach to animals and people. Then the seeds hitch a ride to a new growing place.

Hooks

Goosegrass attached to a jumper

Blown by the Wind

Some seeds float on the wind to a new growing place.

A dandelion flower produces up to 400 seeds.

Each seed has a fluffy parachute that helps it float away from its parent plant.

Dandelion flower

Parachute

Seed

The longer a seed floats in the air, the farther it can travel from its parent plant.

The seeds of a **sycamore** tree have wings like helicopter blades.

The wings help the seeds whirl and spin through the air.

Sycamore seed

Wing

Let's **Test It!**

What shape of seed do you think will float best in the wind?

Gather your equipment and materials:
- A notebook and pen
- Scissors
- Glue
- Craft materials such as beads, feathers, paper, string, modelling clay
- Tape measure

1. Write down your ideas and draw your seed design.

2. Use the materials to make your design.

3. Choose a spot to stand. Place your seed on the palm of your hand. Blow hard on the seed.

How far did the seed travel? Measure the distance and record your result.

What changes would you make to your seed design to help it travel farther?

4. Make your new design and test it!

Eating Seeds and Fruit

Many of the foods we eat are seeds and fruit.

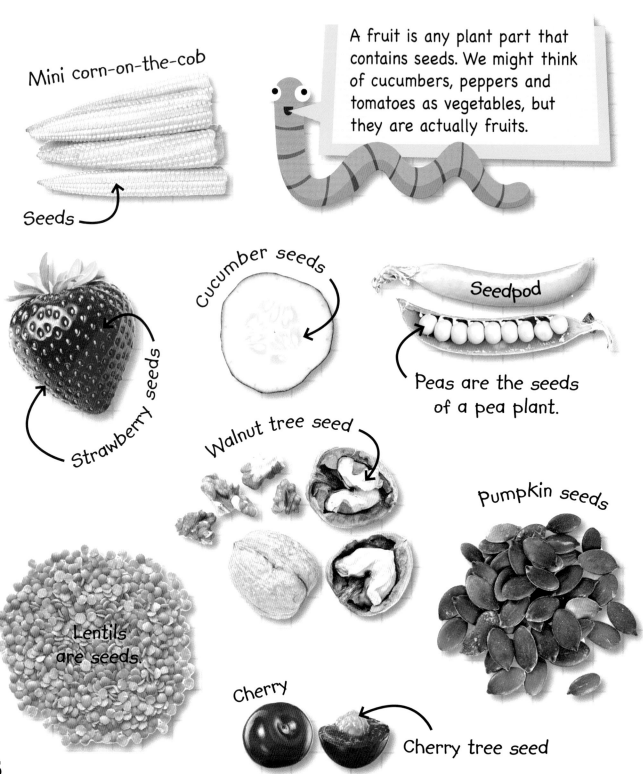

Mini corn-on-the-cob

Seeds

A fruit is any plant part that contains seeds. We might think of cucumbers, peppers and tomatoes as vegetables, but they are actually fruits.

Cucumber seeds

Seedpod

Peas are the seeds of a pea plant.

Strawberry seeds

Walnut tree seed

Pumpkin seeds

Lentils are seeds.

Cherry

Cherry tree seed

Kiwi fruit seeds.

Avocado

Seed

Pepper seeds

A bagel with black poppy seeds

Orange seed

Peanut plant seeds

Have you ever noticed a tiny squiggly part inside a peanut?

This is the part that grows into a new peanut plant.

The peanut plant grows from here.

27

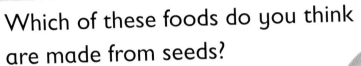

More Seeds to Eat!

Which of these foods do you think are made from seeds?

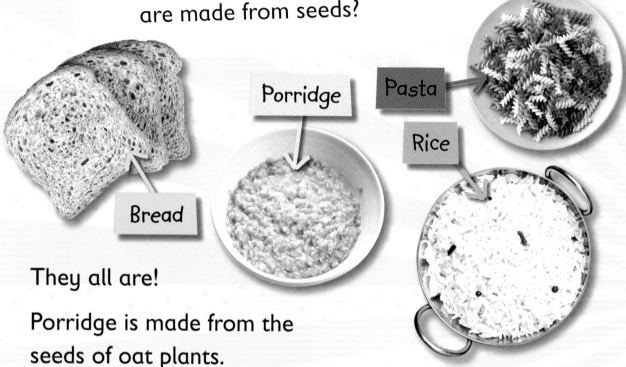

Porridge

Pasta

Rice

Bread

They all are!

Porridge is made from the seeds of oat plants.

When you eat rice, you're eating rice plant seeds.

The seeds of wheat plants are made into flour for baking bread, biscuits and cakes.

Wheat

Wheat seeds are also used to make pasta dough.

The dough is made into shapes using cutters.

Pasta dough

Cutters

Wheat, rice and oats are types of grass plants. The seeds of these plants are known as **grains**.

Check It Out!

What seeds and fruits have you eaten this week?

Make a list in a notebook.

Remember to include foods made from grains.

Toast and strawberry jam

29

From a Tiny Seed

Most seeds fall from their parent plant in summer. They settle in the soil and wait for spring to begin growing.

A dandelion plant grows fast.

It produces leaves, flowers and seeds in just a few weeks.

Dandelion seedling

Dandelion plant

Most trees grow slowly. Some types of trees live for hundreds or even thousands of years!

This is a giant sequoia tree. It is more than 2000 years old and is the largest tree on Earth. It grew from a seed that was smaller than a baked bean!

Glossary

grains
The seeds of grass plants, such as wheat and rice, that people eat.

insect
An animal with six legs, a body in three sections and a hard shell called an exoskeleton.

nectar
A sweet liquid made by flowers.

nutrient
A substance that a living thing needs to grow and be healthy. Plants usually take in nutrients from soil through their roots.

pollen
A coloured dust that is made by flowers and cones, and is needed for making seeds.

roots
Underground parts of a plant that take in water and nutrients from the soil.

seedling
A new, young plant that sprouts from a seed.

shoot
A new part of a plant. Shoots grow from seeds and from existing plants.

Index